THE BEST BRITIS

WITHDRAWN

1 6 JUN 2023

THE
BEST
BRITISH
POETRY
2015

◇   ◇   ◇

EMILY BERRY was born in 1981 in London, where she still lives. She received an Eric Gregory Award in 2008 and is the author of *Dear Boy* (Faber & Faber, 2013), which won the Forward Prize for Best First Collection and the Hawthornden Prize. She is a contributor to *The Breakfast Bible* (Bloomsbury, 2013), a compendium of breakfasts.

RODDY LUMSDEN (born 1966) is a Scottish poet, who was born in St Andrews. He has published six collections of poetry, a number of chapbooks and a collection of trivia, as well as editing a generational anthology of British and Irish poets of the 1990s and 2000s, *Identity Parade*. He lives in London where he teaches for The Poetry School. He has done editing work on several prize-winning poetry collections and edited the Pilot series of chapbooks by poets under 30 for tall-lighthouse. He is organiser and host of the monthly reading series BroadCast in London. In 2010, he was appointed as Poetry Editor for Salt.

THE
BEST
BRITISH
POETRY
2015

◇ ◇ ◇

EMILY BERRY, *Editor*
RODDY LUMSDEN, *Series Editor*

SALT

CROMER

PUBLISHED BY SALT

12 Norwich Road, Cromer, Norfolk NR27 0AX United Kingdom

Printed in Great Britain by Clays Ltd, St Ives plc

Typeset in Bembo 10.5 / 12

ISBN 978 1 78463 030 0 paperback

1 3 5 7 9 8 6 4 2

CONTENTS

Foreword by Roddy Lumsden ix

Introduction by Emily Berry x

Aria Aber, First Generation Immigrant Child 1

Astrid Alben, One of the Guys 2

Rachael Allen, Prawns of Joe 3

Janette Ayachi, On Keeping a Wolf 5

Tara Bergin, The Hairdresser 7

Crispin Best, poem in which i mention at the last moment
an orrery 8

A. K. Blakemore, Poem in which darlings 10

Sarah Boulton, Powder 12

Kit Buchan, The Man Whom I Bitterly Hate 13

Sam Buchan-Watts, 'The days go just like that' 15

Miles Burrows, Letter to an Elderly Poet 16

Niall Campbell, Midnight 17

Vahni Capildeo, Moss, for Maya 18

Kayo Chingonyi, Legerdemain 19

Sophie Collins, Dear No. 24601 20

Claire Crowther, Week of Flies, 1968 22

Paula Cunningham, A History of Snow 23

Jesse Darling, 14 Dreams 25

Patricia Debney, Dream 1 30

Ian Duhig, The Rûm District 32

Joe Dunthorne, Old days 34

Francine Elena, Fish Magic 35

Inua Ellams, Swallow Twice 36

Andrew Elliott, The Storm in American Fiction 38

Victoria Field, Mrs Bagnall Explains Magnesium 39

Annie Freud, Birth Control 40

Matthew Gregory, Decline of the House— 41

David Hart, He wrote 43

Selima Hill, My Father's Smile 44

Sarah Howe, Sirens 45

Kathleen Jamie, The Berries 47

Tom Jenks, from Spruce 48

Luke Kennard, Cain Anagrams 52

Amy Key, Gillingham 54

Kate Kilalea, Sometimes I think the world is just a vast
breeding ground for mosquitoes 56

Caleb Klaces, Genit—   57
Zaffar Kunial, The Word   62
Daisy Lafarge, girl vs. sincerity   63
Melissa Lee-Houghton, i am very precious   65
Dorothy Lehane, Sombrero galaxy   70
Fran Lock, Melpomene   71
Adam Lowe, Vada That   73
Chris McCabe, The Repossessor   75
Amy McCauley, Kadmea Touch Me   77
Alex MacDonald, End Space   79
Andrew McMillan, Ókunna Þér Runna   81
Kathryn Maris, It was discovered that gut bacteria were responsible   82
Sophie Mayer, Silence, Singing   83
Kim Moore, The Knowing   89
Salah Niazi, The Dilemma of al-Kamali   90
Jeremy Over, Artificially Arranged Scenes   94
Bobby Parker, Thank You for Swallowing My Cum   96
Rebecca Perry, apples are ¼ air   97
Holly Pester, The man from Okay   98
Heather Phillipson, Guess what?   99
Padraig Regan, Apples, Cherries, Apricots & Other Fruits
        in a Basket, with Pears, Plums, Robins, a Woodpecker,
        a Parrot, & a Monkey Eating Nuts on a Table   101
Sam Riviere, Preferences   103
Sophie Robinson, where the heart is streaming   105
Jessica Schouela, Poem In Which I Watch Jane Brakhage Give Birth   107
Stephen Sexton, Elegy for Olive Oyl   108
Penelope Shuttle, O blinde Augen   110
Hannah Silva, from The Kathy Doll   111
Marcus Slease, The Underground   113
Greta Stoddart, Letter from Sido   115
Chloe Stopa-Hunt, The Leopard-God   118
Rebecca Tamás, Flame Brocade Moth   119
Jack Underwood, Accidental Narratives   120
Mark Waldron, I am lordly, puce and done,   121
Megan Watkins, Losing Lion   122
Karen McCarthy Woolf, Mort Dieu   123
Samantha Wynne-Rhydderch, Losing It   124

Contributors' Notes and Comments   127
List of Magazines   165
Acknowledgements   168

FOREWORD

by Roddy Lumsden

◊ ◊ ◊

The poems presented in this volume were selected from UK-based poetry magazines, literary journals and online publications issued between spring 2014 and spring 2015. The main purpose of this volume is to celebrate the thriving scene of literary magazines and the developing sphere of literary sites online. For the past twelve months, this year's Guest Editor Emily Berry has been reading these publications as they appeared, seeking poems which she felt should be reproduced here. The format of the book owes a debt to *The Best American Poetry* series of anthologies which was founded in 1988. Similar volumes appear each year in Canada, Australia and Ireland. I would like to offer many thanks to Emily for her work in putting this book together.

INTRODUCTION

by Emily Berry

◇ ◇ ◇

Hi, it's quite scary to be the sole editor of an anthology. On the one hand I said to myself, who am I to be deciding, on my own, what is 'best' (not to mention 'British') out of the thousands of poems published in the UK over a twelve-month period? On the other hand I thought that I was exactly the person to be deciding it. I mean, we all think that whatever we like is the best, right?

For a moment, like previous editors of this anthology, I thought dutifully about the meaning of 'best'. Should I, in selecting the year's 'best' poems, choose poems I liked best or, in some sort of public spirit not entirely natural to me, should I choose poems which I deemed, somehow, objectively best? Even if there is such a thing as objectively best, I knew I wouldn't be capable of stripping away all my biases and predilections to uncover such a thing, so I went with the former. Also because it sounded more fun. And because I wanted to make a little collection of my favourite pebbles that washed up on a particular beach in the Year of Our Lord 2015, put them on a windowsill and invite people to look at and admire them. Welcome.

Instead of thinking about 'best' I started thinking about what it means to like something, because whatever else happened I wanted to like the poems I put in this anthology. I thought about how liking something can be a communal experience, and it can be a private one (it can be both at once): sometimes you like something secretly and you don't want anyone to know about it (maybe you're not sure if other people will also like it, or maybe you just want to keep it to yourself and indulge your own liking of it without interruption); sometimes you like something and you want to have your liking validated by other people's liking, or you want to share your liking. Of course, this is basically a book about the sharing type of liking, but nonetheless I think there may be some of all of these types of likings in here.

Showing people what you like can be daunting because some people will not like the same things you like; I said to myself: What if some of the poems in this book were impulse purchases, like the time I bought a really crazy pointed felt hat? But then I realised I actually couldn't imagine a better anthology than one that was the poetry equivalent of a collection of pointed felt hats.

When I buy a new item of clothing I often think, oh, I should save this for best, but then I end up wearing it all the time. Which means that I have nothing to wear when I need to look 'my best', unless that is to wear what I always like to wear. (But anyway shouldn't something 'best' be something you want with you all the time?) Maybe the poems in this book are poems I intended to keep for special occasions, but ended up wearing every day – and now I invite you to wear them. Anyway I hate special occasions. Except the special occasion of this book, which I love.

THE
BEST
BRITISH
POETRY
2015

◇ ◇ ◇

ARIA ABER

First Generation Immigrant Child

◊　◊　◊

I am the girl in the threesome, sucking and studying
another girl's body, my mind a knot of tinkling beads
tangled inside a stranger's unwashed hands. I am the girl
with the headscarf in the hallway of a mosque, a glassy
bone at my grandfather's funeral, my cousin whispering
through my damp and perfumed hair *Blood is thicker than water,*
even for whores, her breath a verve of Darjeeling and Marlboro
Lights. Sometimes, all I can think of are the playgrounds we
grew up in, even the elm trees smelled of urine and Turkish meat.
I am my father's child, unfurling on the Persian rug as he explains
the world to me, *If at least the Americans or Brits*
had colonised our country, we'd have it easier today. I am
the girl waking at night with sand grains snowing from
the corners of my mouth, but you smile and kiss the sweat,
I know, I know, you dreamt of the desert again. Sometimes, all I can
think of is how the Taliban tortured my mother for being
a feminist, she had to stand for thirty-three days, tongue-dead
and freezing, until her period crawled down her thighs
like the clogged arteries of an ageing heart that beats
a couple of peaks before an infarction, veining the steel
floor with a little warm rivulet. I am an atom in that rivulet,
compounding pain and art and poetry with the velvet odour
of womanhood and politics decaying.

from *Wasafiri*

ASTRID ALBEN

One of the Guys

◇ ◇ ◇

The poet – that ingenious deliverer of ambiguities
leant warmly into me at the festival bar –
lisped through his whisky lips how not too much poetry
should be *done* by *too* many girls. You see, *or elthe!*
poetry and the literary life would lose all credibility.
I asked him how he envisaged achieving this mantopia.
He, startled as a town crier pissing down his pants
intensified his breath, and with the conviction of a fist,
Are you turning, *shurely* not, *feminissshht*? After all, apart
from those – eyes bulging like an antediluvian television screen –
Astrid, you're one of us; and licking the rim of my Babycham
rose from the barstool to hover over me, repeated, you're one of the *guyths*.
This poet in possession of some, localised, repute, dear reader,
I swear to god, he really did believe that he was complimenting me.

from the *Times Literary Supplement*

Prawns of Joe

after Selima Hill

◊   ◊   ◊

When I had a husband I found it hard to breathe.
I was up early he'd get home late
to rub the baby, we took it in turns.
He left, and if someone knocked for him
now at the door, I would not let him go to them.
In amongst all the crying, I see
a burning child on the stove.
The same one as before?
The curtains are full of soot. Well quickly,
we need to escape. Well surely.
No, I watch her burn.

What is it I love about the sound of dogs barking
as smoke rises out the window?
What a complete noise, like a pile of hands clapping.
Another body found burned in the oval,
purple and mystical
and all around her
peppery crisps in the shape of a heart.

There's a woman over the road
who moved in when he left.
She has a black little finger
and has been watching me for days.
Her shadow is that of a man's in the right light.
Sometimes she's right outside the window
sometimes I think she's in the house
in the cupboard under the sink
or behind the shower curtain.
I hold her name like grit between my teeth
turning cartwheels by the edge of the stream.

The air is touchy, fibreglass,
summer streams through the trees like a long blond hair.
I want to grab all the things that make me ashamed
and throw them from the bridge
like how I don't like the sun at the end of the day,
eating cold cream cake on the dimming porch
in the yellow breeze, lonely,
just thinking up these stories.
So I fling my fork into the bark like a stroppy dictator,
it makes that cartoon stuck-in-wood noise.
I am stuck in the middle of the month (again).
I would like to have some time on my hands
something like a stain.
Happy Birthday floats up to my window
followed by your name, your purple name.

from *The Test Centre* and *The Quietus*

On Keeping a Wolf

(for MacGillivray)

◊ ◊ ◊

Like all the therianthropic women that have tapped
Virgil's sorcerer for his poisonous herbs

I keep the wolf chlorinated with friendship
instead of suffocating her with the trappings of love.

The night we met she appeared straight from the page
of a Gaskell gothic tale with metronome footsteps

fire-proof in lace and velvet
engulfing me like a hurricane on its hind legs.

We leaned into each other over a bar-crowd
of people punctuated like rain

our similarities and superstitions centre aligned
we spoke in furious tangential tongues.

Giddy on her smell of clementine peel, argan and tinder
I rested my head back against the chair where I watched

her corset-tight chest rise and fall as she breathed
until brazen-clad in confessional ink we escaped

to smoke cigarettes and kiss
a feral pawing of retractable flames in doorways.

She invited me to her daylight guise
an antique bookshop in the Grass Market

a fitting cove for a wolf where I clasped her book

like a talisman bullet-proof in its hot-print shield

and imagined what the throat of the heart
would sound like after midnight's sober bell.

We played shop, tourists ask for Kipling and whiskey guides
she tells me where her true love is tied:

to a married man she has known an epoch
she grinned a charge of stockings and lost boys

her pupils' plutonian-dark, as black as my mornings
those last thirty days where grey-haired women walked dogs

picked dandelions, tossed sticks along the river of Lethe:
but here, now, she is the white latex of broken stems

an old world language in concertina with the sky,
she is African arrow poison dismantling my pulse
                    and I am running out of places to hide.

from *Oxford Poetry*

The Hairdresser

◇   ◇   ◇

My hairdresser is young
and she tells me things
no one else can:
about the different kinds of straightening tongs;
about the war in Afghanistan.

I sit with my hands in my lap,
in the ridiculous cape that she fastens for me
at the back. She stands at the nape of my neck

and I concentrate.

She tells me about her nan's hair –
which is coarse ('like yours') –
she tells me about colour, and tone;
she tells me about her boyfriend, the soldier,
who covered his ears at the party,
and begged her to take him home.

I watch her in the mirror,
as she cheerfully takes hold of my hair,
and pulls it high up into the air;

I sit completely still in the swivel-chair,
and listen with great care
to all the things she has to tell me.

from the *Times Literary Supplement*

poem in which i mention at the last moment an orrery

◊ ◊ ◊

there are certain
people i have only ever met in
the rain

i am a moon and you
are a moon
i mean i am the moon and yes
you are too
i am calmer when we're the
moon if you can believe such
a thing

consider the things my body is
for example there is a part of it
which is an ankle
another part which i can only describe as
the distance between distance
and distance
a part which makes a muffled
hopeful noise and another part which is
an ankle

on the moon there is an american flag
on us though there is nothing
just now

of the 47 nesting herons
displaced by recent storms
47 died

i have stopped doing the thing you sometimes
complain about
which we notice at the same time
tapioca exists you've just
remembered and so tell me

oh my heavens we think and then
the word tapioca
together

moon and moon
tapioca

all the same there are certain people
i have never met

good morning pop music
is inside me like a wind
pop music is in me like
gas in the moon

there is an orrery
of us
i have seen it behind
glass and it is true

from *Poems in Which*

A. K. BLAKEMORE

Poem in which darlings

◇ ◇ ◇

perhaps it is better this way – this loss
refined through rain –

but they were nine-tails slender in broad daylight and
thin air.   now alone in a car in the dark   i suppose
you thank your blacker stars   and apple pips and wait
for steps to sound across the forecourt and   *Hello, Trouble* breathed
a semi-tone below   the clouds and gravestones like
rows of hunched polonium widows and the reeds – suppose they tremble
as though in pain   and so you turn your face away and   remember
virtue makes for tedious company –

and once you drove. it was an allegory.

the tigerless land gold-fringed green   and green-fringed-blue
where they drew the richness of the world out among   the plaintive waders and
sand twirled in ruins and worm-mounds . . .   the sky   your sheets   and though
his soft dark hair all soaked   straight through.
remember lush mad holding   then say *I did not love him, it was then I knew.*
blood all quiet   vanilla

but accidents generate their own scent   and energy
in-   imicable, escapable   as the skin you burned on boys
who'd broken every toe   and there –   ·
that burning   you smell   before each fainting fit
where you dream

he says your name to you   again

                    from *Poems in Which*

Powder

◊ ◊ ◊

There was a stone cast out all by itself from her installation.
I much preferred the stone to the artwork, in fact to the whole exhibition
which I had been looking forward to seeing immensely.
I picked up the stone, put it in my pocket and took it home with me.
The next day I grated it up into crystalline powder, poured it into a pot
of clear nail varnish and painted my nails. I have some left

from *tender*

The Man Whom I Bitterly Hate

◇　◇　◇

I leave in the evening and waiting for me is a man whom I bitterly hate.
He's staring at me with improbable glee and I gulp as his pupils inflate.
The Saracen's Head is upholstered in red and the whole of his head is a grin
as brindled and coarse as the bones of a horse when he hands me my ginger and gin.

Then after he's kissed me he buries a fist in my belly to tell me I'm late
and with each cigarette that I take I forget he's a man whom I bitterly hate.
The hours relax and then dribble like wax down the walls of his comforting face;
it's evening again when I come to my senses and start to grow sick of the place.

His horrible stories grow boring and gory, his eyes are like holes in the snow
and after a list of his trysts I insist that it's time I was making to go.
He's vividly angered by this like the man-whom-I-bitterly-hate that he is
so I slip out the back after nicking a mac which I later discover is his.

I gingerly labour my way to a neighbouring pub called the Adam and Eve,
I order some gingers and gin and begin to embroider myself in their weave.
With stooping dejection I catch his reflection revealed in the tabletop glaze;
the man whom I bitterly hate has been sitting beside me for two or three days.

I hurry to tell him my wife is unwell on a drip with an oxygen mask
(this wife I confess is a lie, it's a blessing he's never been bothered to ask).
'Your wife is a whiner, I'll buy you a Heineken, mate, the vagina can wait';
with comments like these he reminds me that he's still a man whom I bitterly hate.

He hefts a guitar from the top of the bar and he calls for the communal ear,
the man whom I bitterly hate is as shit a guitarist as any you'll hear,
it's people are strange in the chelsea the chain hallelujah the passenger sing
she's buying a stairway imagine there's where is my mind we're the sultans of swing,

The Cellar, The Swan on the Green, The Queen Mary, The Edinburgh Castle, The Hen
The Duchess of Cornwall, The Fawn, The Endeavour, The Duchess of Cornwall again,
The Eminent Freighter, The Man Whom I Bitterly Hate, The Trafalgar, The Gun –
I flee him but each time I flee him I see him; he's drinking in every last one.

'You're running away like a snivelling gay!' he accuses, 'What's wrong with you, mate?'
'I bitterly hate you!' I bitterly cry to the man whom I bitterly hate.
He doesn't seem knocked off his perch by this shock information I've longed to reveal,
but he stands on my toes with his lips at my nose and his breathing is all I can feel:

'If I were a traitor like you I'd be grateful for each fucking friend I could get;
Your life only goes unassaulted cos no one's decided to ruin it yet.'
With this unexpectedly sinister threat in my ears I arrive at my gate
which swings with a clattering giggle like that of the man whom I bitterly hate.

I cling to the side of my fictional bride and I drop off to sleep with a shove
but he's there at the seams of my pitiful dreams having sex with the people I love.
I'm openly vexed when I wake to his text on my pillow at quarter to eight;
I leave in the evening and waiting for me is a man whom I bitterly hate.

from *Five Dials*

SAM BUCHAN-WATTS

'The days go just like that'

◇ ◇ ◇

If you emerge from the glove of woods –
the trail's patchiness like jaundiced spliff-paper
and the dry powder bloom of a fire extinguisher
let off by kids last night –
blinking, feeling skew-whiff, confused, to find this:
a medieval re-enactment *in medias res*
then you have seen it exactly as it should be seen,
exposed, but distant, so that the quirks –
the radiant tinkle, the gathers of enthusiasts,
the rhubarb-rhubarbs, the unintelligible frills,
the coarseness of sound their make-shift dress makes
like brown paper crumpling as it's being burnt –
are so correct, as if history were a thing to be administered
amidst the afternoon. And the hold-all blue
seems about to decompress, until all we have left
is a far-off clobber of wood. And the days go just like that.

from *Poetry London*

MILES BURROWS

Letter to an Elderly Poet

◇ ◇ ◇

Better to be writing your will again,
To be feasting in the great hall by firelight
Playing the harp to your grandchildren.
What is that terrible cry at the end of the garden?
It has gone now.
Could have been birds. Wild geese perhaps.
Let your trembling hand draw an expressive line.
Consider the scuffs on the risers to the stairs,
The dent of the doorknob hitting the wall
Always at the same place. Unpurse your lips.
You are not writing prescriptions.
Nor falling downstairs in a foreign language.
Practise the smile of the Indian swami.
Relax, your rivals are dead.
At least you're not in a Mexican motel.
Hang up the picture of a Chinese sage
Sweeping things under an enormous rock.

from *PN Review*

Midnight

◇   ◇   ◇

My heart had been repeating *oh heart, poor heart*
all evening. And all because I'd held my child,
oh heart, and found that age was in my cup now;

poor heart, it bare knew anything
but the life of a young axman in the forest,
whistler, tree-feller, swinging with the wind,

where *oh heart, poor heart* isn't the heard song,
where there is no cry in the night, no cradling,
no heart grown heavy, heavier, with caring.

from *Poetry London*

VAHNI CAPILDEO

Moss, for Maya

for Maya Chowdhry

◇ ◇ ◇

I. A child left alone can befriend moss. Its bright green, enticing to
the eye as a lemon lolly behind the teeth, makes moss seem to shine
in the darkness under lizard-haunted ixora bushes & on the killing
patch of concrete that disaffected workmen splashed on earth that
had been alive with wet-combed roots, as if extermination were
necessary for human habitation, & moss an infiltrator.

II. Moss has not tiny tongues, nor little fingers, nor flames fine as
watchmakers' tools, nor an elfin semaphore system. Moss is not-
lockable, not-glossolalia, not in-the-way-on-the-way. Moss is
myriad, simply many & one. Moss absorbs.

III. For the benefit of giants, fourteen kinds of Icelandic moss were
exhibited under glass, including the static flicker of a moss named
for its resemblance to white worms, a name mistranslatable
as 'pale dragons'. It must have been plucked from the cooled
flowing lava fields that look like nothing, yet where detail thrives
– clumps of pink carnivorous daisies, trapping zippy insect life.

IV. The life cycle of moss is momentous. Any given colony of moss
could have been there since whichever chosen beginning, while
changing at a rate that puts mammals' eyes to shame.

V. Don't slip. Grab the balustrade. Don't slip. She's broken her arm.
Don't scrape too much off. It's beautiful. Bleach it all off. It's a
risk. Coexist. Moss exists. Our stone selves roll on different tracks,
unmatchably cracked. We cling. Resist. Shape to our ends whatever
is. Not this. Moss induces words in us because, grave & new, we
sentence things; whereas moss carpets, respires, pulls back, is.

from *clinic*

Legerdemain

◇ ◇ ◇

and, at last, you have come upon
the jewel in the crown of our collection
here at the Royal Museum for Central Africa:
a magnifying glass used by one
of the King's functionaries
who, by Royal decree, remained
unsung among the sons of Europe
until recently. Note the engraving
on the ivory handle that tells us
this glass was used in the Kasai.
Since the official report was redacted
some of you might be unaware
of this particular brand of magic:
the 'trick was to use a magnifying
glass to light a cigar, "after which
the white man explained his intimate
relation to the sun, and declared
that if he were to request [the sun]
to burn up his black brother's
village it would be done"''*
and so it was the land changed hands
as a cigar, given light, becomes a stub
and its smoke that stays with you
is the smoke from a burning village.

from the *Morning Star*

* George Washington Williams as quoted in *King Leopold's Ghost* by Adam Hochschild

Dear No. 24601

◇   ◇   ◇

The future is an eye that I don't dare look into
Last night I dreamed I was a ball of fire
and woke up on the wrong side of the room
This is a recurring dream
I share an apartment with my twin sister
Enclosed is a photo of us on a tandem bike
I forget which one I am
Sometimes I wake up believing I am her
she is me
and there is nothing about the day to indicate otherwise
Weeks stack up this way
As a girl I did not do well with other children
Unable to see the fun in games
I paid close attention to the weather
delighting in hail and not much else
save a prized collection of Hummel figurines
derived from the pastoral sketches
of Sister Maria Innocentia Hummel
German Franciscan nun and talented artist
Her simple peaceful works
drew the enduring hatred of Hitler himself
You know Hummel translates as *bumblebee* in German
and they say she was always 'buzzing' around
What do you think do we grow into our names
or does kismet know a thing
One name can mean too much
the other not nearly enough
The small things make a difference
like sitting on the white cushion
as opposed to the blue
white is pure of course

but my soul's been in the bargain bin since Russia
and Lenin's tomb
I had a moment there
among the balustrades
and once that moment had expired
it graduated
from a moment to a life

from *The White Review*

Week of Flies, 1968

◊ ◊ ◊

A spray, 'Finito', was at our disposal.
We were urged to use it and not to crush them
against the walls or ceiling, to take care

to switch lights off before opening windows,
to excuse authorities for the success
of spiders escaping into our house:

'We must afford an invasion of insects
 coming from the lake. They do not sting.'

I dressed in a black cloak. We swarmed unguarded
offices. Alsatians chased us and we lived
on free soup cooked up in Europe's cities.

from *Shearsman*

A History of Snow

◊　◊　◊

It was wild sudden.
Her daddy phoned me to work.
She was that hot he just had a sheet over her.
I felt the heat before I lifted the sheet and seen the rash.

You'd never forget that rash.
People say to me 'How would you know?'
and I just say 'You'd know if you seen it.'
Purple.

The wee spots and these big blotches like birthmarks –
everywhere only her face.
Her wee lady and all.
I phoned and they said do the glass test.

I pressed really hard
and her bawling, but it didn't change
so we brung her up.
There was this old man in the queue

very wheezy, he said to the girl
'I want them to see this child
before they see me.'
And within two minutes we're in the ambulance.

She was bouncing up and down on the trolley,
you wouldn't believe it. Like something
out of *The Exorcist*. The doctor come
and he told us prepare for the worst.

She's a bit of hearing loss, that's all,
in big rooms, like, but she's grand.
They say it'll all come right, the ear adjusts.
Her daddy brung her snow in a lunchbox –

she'd never seen it before.
They'd pushed her cot right up to the window,
the flakes sweeping past like confetti,
a bit of a rose in her cheeks, and her all eyes.

The cars in the car park were buried in minutes,
it was one snowy evening, the whole
of the country froze. She'd been in four weeks
and I mind she was eating an orange –

a mandarin one of the nurses had peeled.
That's when I knew she really was on the mend.
They said if we'd even been five minutes later.
I think of that old man yet.

from *PN Review*

14 Dreams

◇ ◇ ◇

A great white shark is huge, makes Jaws look like shit. He's a lumbering monster with a mouth like vagina dentata & his blubber rolls out like the hugest penis, ugh. No wide ocean but channelled thin canals, above which a series of rickety walkways are built; it all has to be on stilts and this for various logistical reasons, not least of which the great white shark. It's some kind of prom or a celebration of parochial well-nested import and my dad is there in a suit, I have to intercept him, do I strike him? Probably he's drunk. I call the heavies in, and as I leave I tell em be gentle. Thin line between love and hate anyway. Art space on hell sticks and we're talking about the work, which is nowhere visible; it's meta-architectural. In the top corner, as with doctors' waiting rooms, there's a little telly playing art porn: I recognise the subtitles and credits as my parents start moving towards the grave. An S&M musical ballet, everyone singing and syncopated: there are thin women in Nazi military gear and the TV isn't art either. In the film a woman engages intimately with an animate organ, some great big clump of whatever with a supple soft centre. She's putting her face in it, she's putting her hands in it. Oh gosh, she says. Fruity posh voice. Mmm, oh gosh. She comes. Sorry, she says. Gosh. Someone says I should have had children earlier. Ironic, says a woman in a Nazi suit. Mmm, says the woman in the film.

I'm riding my horse off the ferry into the cold mountain road down Coney Island. The full head of Lady Liberty is lit up w the dawn, looming large over the hill it's not a true Coney it's another. She seems to be exploding but maybe thas jus what it looks like when they spark her torch up. I take pictures on my iPhone, knowing they'll like the image over on Instagram. I'm riding my horse very much. We ride through a snowy Coney with nothing open but a rubber-smelling drug hustler boy's coffee shop staffed by a soft-voiced exhausted Polish girl and the gift shop cum breakfast bar, beacons in the cold steaming scent of inferior bacon fat & shrink-wrapped pastries being baked out of their packets sweet acrid artificial butter & vanilla. I'm in love with my horse and then I'm drinking with someone. Chubby, with dark hair, voluble when drunk; one of those things where you kiss and go home together after all, but doesn't it feel like that's the natural conclusion of every long night drinking? The whole thing feels like a hangover.

Elsewhere: a long table, a feast, feuds laid to rest in a mud world under a non-blue non-sky heaven; a new lover. It's nobody I know but a young man who kills birds for food. We're sitting in the trenches with a child and its parents and we're all laughing but I'm nervous, scratching at the mud. I dig up something heavy and metallic: a bullet case someone once made into a capsule for precious things. An old pound coin falls out and the child reaches to grab it. His father is stern: excuse me, mister, you don't know where that's been. His mother says look, somebody died here, that once belonged to them. We all exchange grown-up looks and say something about the past and the present. When I wake up it occurs to me that all the knowing adults I knew as a child were only playing at being knowing adults, and that nobody really knew anything at all: the true legacy is the horror and the failure of all them went before.

There's been a murder, maybe, and due to the nature of the murder everyone's getting kids on the case – Scotland Yard, the whole nine. Something about how children process data, something about how they intuit signs, something about something only kids can see. Nobody's happy about this state of affairs but everybody admits it's the only way. At some point – admittedly a bad moment – my old lover shows up, or his voice does, saying: 'I pack light.' I've heard this before and I'm in no mood for rationalisation. I don't dream about you anymore, I say, and he disappears.

My sister gives away a present she bought for me and I meet my old art teacher sitting on a bench. I'm getting old, he says. Me too, I say: me too. About fifteen years since I saw the guy and time can do a lot. 'Danger is related to the size of things,' says a patronising voiceover, 'a jack knife for a baby is potentially fatal; an elephant might not even feel it.'

It's a really cold day in an unfamiliar town, flea markets and sleety rain. I'm sick numb heartbroken from visiting the house of my ex-lover's ex-lover so I'm looking for power objects and practising being the cat that walks by itself. I need a suit, I think: no more lil tomboy, I'm gonna become a real man, a gentle man. So I go to the flea market, army surplus and morning formal, and I ask the guy if he's got my size. He's a big rough red-headed market carny, an archetype. Suddenly, in amongst all this dead cloth, I'm overcome by sad exhaustion and I sink to my knees; with my eyes still closed I feel an arm around my shoulder, a hand stroking my face. Then the vendor is kissing me and it's very soft. I say how did you know it was okay to touch me? And he said darling I knew it from the minute you walked in here, so we go back to his place. It's a draughty warehouse with a loft bed and a wood stove, and it smells like damp and mildew where the suits are kept over coals in a big morgue oven. But it's clean and spare in the way that men who live alone tend to keep their houses, and I sense he's been alone for a long time. He looks rough but his touch is soft with longing and loneliness, the disbelief of a hand on skin after all this time, tentative and hungry cos the flesh is willing though the heart is broken. Maybe he's death, with his morgue oven and his lonely clothes. Maybe this is what dying will be like. It's not so bad. None of the fire of living love, but a soft and scaly desire that stirs a sleeping animal deep beneath the skin. And breathing in the dark, and the smallest of sighs.

And now with grown-ups except that I'm not, first time at a party feeling, can't let anyone know that my body has never felt this way before on strange drugs and unfamiliar emotions and the dizzy sick of first cigarettes. I know I'm handsome, but I'm scared of the older women looking at me and I wish I knew how to be pretty like the pretty lady and hoping someone will come and put their arm around me. It was 9/11 and there were 10 red planes crashing in balletic formation and it brought down half of Brooklyn. A hilltop highway more like France or California on fire or maybe it was just some street in Anywhere City and I was young, younger, getting packed off to somewhere with all my bags in the back of a car with a boy, a brother maybe or a crush or cousin, and soon after the punchline which was a twist so huge and whole that putting words to it is just a killing act but I want to keep it though it's already lost.

Waves breaking on the turquoise tiles of ancient beaches, flooding, seepage, rain, a storm. A love story, violent in its complexity. You are all there somewhere. Tears, more water, sex: 'you wanna see the real Venezia?' Leering in, but yes, I do. I'm rocking like a boat, so hard it wakes me up.

The rings of Saturn are like a conveyor belt that spins faster and faster and faster and faster, vroom.

Started talking to the bear-shaped biscuit pickle I was about to put in my mouth like sorry didn't realise, are you okay? With the heavy dignity of one used to generations of persecution the bear biscuit replied that [he] was, and thanked me for noticing. Something something happy swimming something something holiday brine. The bear is now a power centre and granted rights to life and language will take over the world. It suggests that swimming in seawater is a form of self-marinade, that we too will pickle up nicely. Seamless plotline that crescendoed in a wow moment when 100 little glass ponies in US airbase military formation circled the perfect ankles of a blonde beach goddess as though conjured; and all I have is the same feeling I had when I was little and first heard the word 'palomino' and then later when I read the illustrated *Black Beauty* and there were My Little Ponies everywhere, and something about horses and ponies being so fabulous and libidinal like drag queens like I never wanted or wanted to be a rock star but I think I wanted and wanted to be a horse.

Hot dusty world and a hot dirty love story in which I'm the androgyne outlaw and she's my submissive blonde ingenue. We're on the run, we don't stop moving; a series of family-run rural hotels with restaurants where we do it in the dining room and people look askance. But this is our delinquency – there's rage in it, there's righteousness and brightness and lust in it, there ain't no stopping us now. At some point we're on a boat. We don't stop drinking either and we're woozy and handsy, tired out from travelling and sex when we see the crocodile. He is majestic, massive, but he's dying. We become obsessed with this crocodile. We stay in this town just to watch him every day. He fills us with weird feelings, erotic unease. We discover that there's a youngish lady vet who wrangles him out of the water to give him his meds, and we become obsessed with her too – the act of shoving something down this crocodile's throat. One day after watching the crocodile I go to one of the rural parlours and get a huge tattoo of red lattice scales in his honour; it starts at my shoulder blade and continues right up the side of my face. Briefly I wonder if this was a good idea and my heart sinks when I realise it's there for good. But soon I don't care about the tattoo any more cos my lil girl is by my side & she can't get enough of me and we're back on the road, in and out of bed, and onwards.

A young girl becomes pathologically fixated on some dark magical aspect of sex; it begins with her own lover, who then disappears, and after that she wants mine. My lover is a man and I'm not really me either. She's in the hallway outside our room, breathing hard and turning herself inside out, insatiable, implacable. We're all naked. I tell him to go fuck her if he wants, and he bounds out with an erection in an attitude of I-don't-mind-if-I-do. But then he's gone too. It's as though she has eaten him, but nothing so visceral; he has just disappeared, never to return again. It becomes a sexual stand-off: I'm the only living thing left, and she wants me, body and soul. I don't give in. She masturbates herself into virtual nothingness: she is nothing now but a plastic bag on the floor, yet still she thrashes and writhes. I stand on the bag and address it directly. It's a domination scene; some kind of consensual power-play in which both parties somehow get off, though I don't know what happens in the end, or if either of us make it out alive. Slippery plastic, the bag rustles under my feet and I almost lose my balance, like standing on sand when the tide pulls out.

A family-run hotel with puce bruisey carpets in the foy-ay and long cold dorm rooms no better than a scout hut, and groups of West London teens coming tout ensemble for a love-in, all very polite when they get the keys but one reckons it'll be wall-to-wall debauchery once they bring the drugs back. The whole world's a migraine, someone says. My mum's in the observatory, on whose roof a miniature statue of liberty. And it's a beautiful sky like the Lion OsX background, fleshy pale galaxial labial, a big salivary whitewash in the split centre of a sky wet with stars. I'm spacing out while others are talking; I hold up my hands to make a bird shadow and I give the statue of liberty wings. I'm smiling awkwardly from holding back tears of wonder. How lovely a thing can be.

A swimming pool, a sunbeam, a pretty girl with a little son, a 50-year-old cake with my sister's name on it, an elderly woman who pushes past me on a narrow brocaded ladder platform to jump to her death because she's 'ready'. In general it's beautiful. There's a lion too. I remember a bodega selling coffee on the upper east side in a hot muggy dawn: am I dreaming New York or is New York dreaming me. A last memory of the barn, and all was painted black.

from *tender*

Dream 1

◊ ◊ ◊

All the literary figures
of my acquaintance
appear to me:

        today
        we have a bite
        to eat

        representations
            respectful as butlers
        whisper in my ear

        while beyond the table
            there's illness
        in another room

I can manage
like this
instructions heeded

doors closed
amid general jollity
and coffee

only then

you take up
residence
in a sunken chair

and all the literary figures
of my acquaintance
nod politely:

        one pulls out a notebook
               ostentatiously
        someone else

        makes you an offer –
               you take his tooth
        in your hand

        this is what you did want
               once
        it's clear

        but now

        you deliberately let it roll
               across the dry skin
        of your palm

                         to the floor

        from *Litmus*

The Rûm District

◇ ◇ ◇

It was there for the taking:
the Emperor's soldiery drunken; its golden birds
flown; mosaics dropping from walls;
iconoclastic barbarians at the gate
already calling this world *Rûm*.

Rûm gave its name to Romania.
Romanian wannabe, I holiday at Bucharest's
Grand Hotel Abyss but find myself
watching television – that very word
a cocktail of Greek and Latin, like Rûm.

But the hotel set's picture seems made
of tesserae rather than pixels,
and its only channel National Geographic
commending whatever is begotten,
born and torn to pieces.

I plunder the minibar, then under the influence
of Xavier de Maistre
embark on a little room travel of my own,
sailing the New Jerusalem of my rented cube
from Revelation through the night of Rûm.

I dream of the poet Rûm calls Rumi,
who tells me the Arabic word for house
names an Arabic poem's unit,
then I wake up in this stanza,
my head spinning like a dervish.

Stanza meaning room, I ring room service
for the hair of the dog, ordering this

rûm cocktail which arrives with an orange slice,
an ash berry, and an ice cube
melting like this poem.

from *The Poetry Review*

Old days

◇   ◇   ◇

Remember when everyone on earth
was pregnant except for you
which was a miracle

and the babies jangled down on their cords
like oxygen masks during unplanned
cabin decompression

and all language was lost to the cutesy voice.
Woo are so wucky, everyone explained,
while you adopted

the brace position, amazed at the serenity
that comes from looking after
yourself.

from the *London Review of Books*

Fish Magic

◇ ◇ ◇

Marisa explained that orchids are a natural technology
and that our technology is what makes us human.
Matthew replied that petals were once leaves
that decided to behave more beautifully.

Today a telephone can be a tropical
fish tank. You appeared so close
the other side of cold glass
after fifteen blue months.

We spoke to each other
for two hours, clarity
broken by glitches,
shoals of yellow tang.

The line *I'm kissing you*
and verse 40 of *Kuruntokai*,
its monsoon meeting red earth,
run through the novel I'm reading.

I understand the image of the kurinji,
blooming once every twelve years in green
shola forest, is a warm, integral part of the poem,
although the plant itself is never mentioned explicitly.

from *Poetry London*

Swallow Twice

◇ ◇ ◇

Given the smallest prompt, Father will describe
how I skulked just beyond the lamplight's reach

watching the ring of men ripe with beer and laughter
push thick fingers into the mountain of spiced meat

roasted with onions, ginger and chillies like an altar
I fought to worship at, swiping through their arms

at the chunks – a mouse attempting to feast with kings.
Frustrated, Father stopped their speech

so I could reach in, greedily choose the choicest piece,
ignore his warnings and tear at the muscle, strain

against the flesh till its elasticity slipped my fingers
and the chunk, chillies and all slapped into my eyes.

Father thumped my back as I coughed on the pepper
/ swallow twice / he urged, dropping the wailing mess

of me on Mother's knees. What Father didn't know
is I imagined the key to their impenetrable talk

lay in the cubed meat and I longed to be like them.

In the circle of friends I have, most of our conversations
revolve around music, the heft and sway of the changing

world, the rapid rate of our redundance, how best
to pretend we know it all and when beer loosens

what inhibitions are left after shredding meat
with bare fingers, laughter cloaks our weaknesses:

our inability to provide for those we love, who love us,
we who still know nothing of what our lovers want,

how frightening it is to have nephews growing up,
who want to be like us, like men.

from *Oxford Poetry*

The Storm in American Fiction

◇　◇　◇

Without necessarily stopping she'll look up from what she is doing
and see across the bedroom wall, falling slower
than she'd have thought a thing could fall,
the shadow, made by the moon, of a maple leaf blown
from the tree before being swept across the floor and vanishing

under the bed like something belonging to her husband
– whose tongue is in her cunt, whose cock is in her mouth –
the loss of which will drive him to turn upside down the house
like the wind may yet the tree and drive away their children
if it weren't for whom she'd have left him and gone to find herself.

from *Sonofabook*

VICTORIA FIELD

Mrs Bagnall Explains Magnesium

◇ ◇ ◇

In fourth-year Chemistry, I had eyes only for Mandy.
I admitted not impediments like Bunsen burners,
the Periodic Table, our teacher with her pink nylon house-coat
and unfamiliar Northern accent. When Mrs Bagnall said,
'soft metal', I felt myself fall into Mandy's burnished copper
curls, my fat fourteen-year-old heart beating like a dead-blow
hammer under an unfamiliar bra. When she made us write
'alkali' in our exercise books, my hand shook at the lingual
looseness of the *l*s, the implied kiss of the *k*. When Mrs Bagnall
called for silence, put on her safety goggles, tucked her hairnet
behind her ears, I held my breath as the blue flame leapt.
She gripped the grey strip with her tongs, paused for effect,
raised the metal ribbon high, then plunged it into the heat.
Mandy yawned slowly, only half-covering the lush, wet redness
of her mouth. The magnesium blazed with a light so white
and so bright, the rest of us gasped, and I nearly died.

from *The Dark Horse*

Birth Control

for my father

◊   ◊   ◊

'This really ought to be simply
                    the most marvellous thing,
                                        but aren't words strange?

Birth after all,
                what could be better than
                                    the beginning of a life?

And control, necessary for everything
                that life has to offer and incidentally
                                    one of my favourite things.'

from *Poetry London*

MATTHEW GREGORY

Decline of the House—

◊ ◊ ◊

i

TOURZEL, LOUISE-ELISABETH-FÉLICITÉ-FLEUR-
MARIE-THÉRÈSE-CHARLOTTE-etc, etc, MARQUISE
DE (1749–1832)

ii

Any given day a gold plate
of songbirds, upwards of fifty
varieties of tarte and cheese,
critical bowel ailments.

The king was fond of locksmithing.
He dreamt in whole escritoires
where locks unlocked
other inscrutable locks.

iii

After days running the stag and boar through
the purple forests of Fontainebleau
he'd crash out in bed. One or other mistress
of his would present herself in undress

before they'd lay in brace, a plucked peacock
and the lion of France. *Majesté is back*
was the word under the white reliefs
of all the court salons. In bed he yawned

widely and Mlle. saw how ruinous his teeth
had become. She scented their world
braided into his breath, like a composition

opening with a sweet, brief movement
of perfume, lawns and the *fêtes galantes*—
closing on dead airs, in rotten ballrooms.

from *Ambit*

He wrote

◇   ◇   ◇

He wrote his dying notes, aha, aha,

    a note in the night, a note at dawn if dawn it was,
    if dawn or lamp, if note it was, written or only thought,
aha alone, aha, aha.

There is a door but not that door, not his door now,
the out of doors not his but different now, rebuilt but not to
celebrate his being gone, where he left his door ajar, ah ha.

Lord for thy tender mercy's sake, lay not our sins . . . he'd say, ah ha,
Dear God and Father of mankind, lay not our sins . . . ah ha,
God be in my head, – and would tap his bald, his well-scratched.

from *The Poetry Review*

SELIMA HILL

My Father's Smile

◊   ◊   ◊

He smiled with the smile of a man
undisturbed by love and its indignities

whom nothing can deflect from his path
of being perfect till the end of time.

from *The Poetry Paper*

Sirens

◊   ◊   ◊

pickerel, n.1 – *A young pike; Several smaller kinds of N. American pike.*
pickerel, n.2 – *A small wading bird, esp. the dunlin,* Calidris alpina.

I see it clearly, as though I'd known it myself,
        the *quick look* of Jane in the poem by Roethke –
that delicate elegy, for a student of his thrown
        from a horse. My favourite line was always *her*
sidelong pickerel smile. It flashes across her face
        and my mind's current, that smile, as bright and fast
and shy as the silvery juvenile fish – glimpsed,
        it vanishes, quick into murk and swaying weeds –
a kink of green and bubbles all that's left behind.

I was sure of this – the dead girl's vividness –
        her smile unseated, as by a stumbling stride –
till one rainy Cambridge evening, my umbrella
        bucking, I headed toward Magdalene to meet an
old friend. We ducked under The Pickerel's
        painted sign, its coiled fish tilting; over a drink
our talk fell to Roethke, his pickerel smile, and
        I had one of those blurrings – glitch, then focus –
like at a put-off optician's trip, when you realise

how long you've been seeing things wrongly.
        I'd never noticed: in every stanza after the first,
Jane is a bird: wren or sparrow, *skittery pigeon.*
        The wrong kind of pickerel! In my head, her
smile abruptly evolved: now the stretched beak
        of a wading bird – a stint or purre – swung
into profile. I saw anew the diffident stilts
        of the girl, her casting head, her gangly almost
grace, puttering away across a tarnished mirror

of estuary mud. In Homer, the Sirens are winged
          creatures: the Muses clipped them for their failure.
By the Renaissance, their feathers have switched
          for a mermaid's scaly tail. In the emblem by Alciato
(printed Padua, 1618) the woodcut pictures a pair
          of chicken-footed maids, promising mantric truths
to a Ulysses slack at his mast. But the *subscriptio*
          denounces women, *contra naturam*, plied with hind-
parts of fish: *for lust brings with it many monsters*.

Or take how Horace begins the *Ars Poetica*,
          ticking off poets who dare too much: mating savage
with tame, or snakes with birds, can only create such
          horrors, he says, as a comely waist that winds up
in a black and hideous fish. The pickerel-girl swims
          through my mind's eye's flummery like a game
of perspectives, a corrugated picture: fish one way
          fowl the other. Could it be that Roethke meant
the word's strange doubleness? *Neither father*

nor lover. A tutor watches a girl click-to the door
          of his study with reverent care, one winter evening –
and understands Horace on reining in fantasy.

from *The Poetry Review*

The Berries

◊ ◊ ◊

When she came for me
through the ford, came for me
through running water
I was oxter-deep in a bramble-grove
glutting on wild fruit. Soon
we were climbing the same
sour gorge the river fled, fall
by noiseless fall. I mind
a wizened oak
cleaving the rock it grew from,
and once, a raptor's mewl.
Days passed – or what passed for days,
and just as I'd put the whole misadventure
down to something I ate,
she leapt twice, thrice, my sick
head spun, and here we were:
a vast glen ringed by snow-peaks,
sashaying grass, a scented breeze,
and winding its way toward us
that same world-river –
its lush banks grazed by horses, horses
I knew she'd leave me for,
right there, her own kin –
no use my pleas, no use
my stumbling back down
to where the berries grew,
because this is what I wanted,
so all I could do was brace myself
and loosen my grip from her mane.

from the *New Statesman*

from *Spruce*

◇　◇　◇

do not eat the berries by the Build A Bear Workshop
the berries by the Build A Bear Workshop are poisonous
no-makeup selfie in the clearance aisle

a stag glimpsed amongst the coleslaw
in the overspill car park where the shamans are
salmon in the standing pools

I will meet you by the memorial bush
I will meet you on the sacred mound
got an amulet and a rotisserie chicken

★

the weight of the potato before it is cooked
the weight of the potato after it is cooked
the weight of the world in mirrored water

in a magical mirror her occult third eyebrow
on the back of a spoon in a chemical toilet
once more the emperor slips into slumber

back at the Gatsby-themed Tupperware party
when I was spammed by a future world champion
in a mobile library on the shores of a loch

★

the incredible story of a truly brave pigeon
in congress by the tower of mincemeat
meteors above the designer outlet

in a walk-in larder the sacred herbs
the Yorkshire terriers will guide you home
down the green lanes in the year of the stoat

two arcs on linoleum intersecting
like ley lines at the organic cheesemonger
like a fun fight at the fondue factory

★

an unhatched egg at Gulliver's World
Piers Morgan refers obliquely to Lenin
buttered bagels at the mausoleum

a lukewarm peach at the webinar
six bulbs blazing one extinguished
yellow leaves green leaves white vinegar red salt

muted kerfuffle in the arboretum
a marital aid in the druid's copse
they found a solution to the monkey puzzle trees

★

in the halls of St Luke a garden suburb
a bird flew through and was noted in the minutes
leakage from headphones in industrial units

redolent blossom a cache of brie
bags of charcoal in sheltered housing
yellow hoods at the business park

on her birthday with champagne grapefruit
in a dream she obstructed the driver's door
scrambled egg on the family crest

★

sleek on leopard print an infomercial
rampant bullfinch rendered metaphorically
in the lobby the imponderable owls

a shaft of air surrounds you Mabel
here in the greenwood with a gastric band
down the log flume the ancient frigate

in the evening we have scant reception
sunken precincts of the lost domain
England through the casement green and miniature

★

on a narrowboat holiday with the cast of *Glee*
we are communists now we share the shower gel
eggs Benedict and soufflé Monte Cristo

herons high above the Travelodge
the vanished wash bag of Raymond Queneau
a stack of unordered pink marshmallows

drone of abandoned mobility scooters
somewhere beneath the dome of the forest
out there immaculate the sarcasm of rooks

★

got his top off on his LinkedIn profile
at the Challenge Cup final they are all wearing towels
in the long gardens repeating rhododendrons

I am battling daemons my addiction to salami
at the leisure centre with the shaolin monks
in the soft play area with the IBS sufferers

I'd like an office in the palm of my hand
what are some things that fool people all the time?
what are some of the most mind-blowing facts about Switzerland?

★

dance-off at the pop-up podiatrist
six blue mink in the municipal treehouse
an array of poodles grandly named

clipped close and lost in the laurel
got a letter printed in *Take A Break*
badly dubbed at the water cooler

in an unseen episode of *Eldorado*
he is in the wine bar in linen slacks
at the salon with a bucket of quiche

★

slightly foxed by a particular nook
I was writing the ransom notes out in longhand
in the vestibule with an implacable bullock

a flash mob of disgruntled accountants
by the partially functioning mini roundabout
bird cloud as the birds ascend

there amongst the bottled plums
with an antelope that triggers the sensors
with a lo-cal tiramisu you will find me

from *The Wolf*

Cain Anagrams

◇ ◇ ◇

An excerpt from a sequence of 31 perfect anagrams of Genesis 4: 9–13 in which
Cain shares an apartment with Father K. in a disputed territory.

Genesis 4: 9–13

And the Lord said unto Cain, Where is Abel thy brother? And he said, I
know not: Am I my brother's keeper? And He said, What hast thou done?
the voice of thy brother's blood crieth unto Me from the ground. And
now art thou cursed from the earth, which hath opened her mouth to
receive thy brother's blood from thy hand; When thou tillest the ground,
it shall not henceforth yield unto thee her strength; a fugitive and a vaga-
bond shalt thou be in the earth.

★

Cain and Father K. share a property. A hutch in the suburb of bachelor-
hood. Overhung by cheesecloth, shoehorned with mutton & things reab-
breviated. The hairy household mythologist & his adherent undertow.
Ornamentation: a hat, bunch of rhododendrons. Diadem the width of
a yacht; Oh, seventeenth endowment. Don't try to thwart a stammered
buffet. This, the trillionth interlude. The buttonhook will have his thread,
the drogue, her logorrhea.

★

Father K. & Bourbon in the bathtub. Why, that escalated fast! Whenever
he unhands it, he shivers. I say we are unthinkably connected. His retort:
a wooded Tarot rant, third odour hushed with boyhood horrors. Never
seen death that uncompetitive. Get uninterpreted blancmange, FWD:
hearth light. Ah, rhombohedral monolith to the hundredth motherhood!
Ah, tenth cheetah hemorrhaging by domed foothills! A cloud of flies, their
toothy neurons out.

We enroll at HRH Ethelred University at Adah's behest. Cain has taken
10 evening modules:
Arsehole Theory
Misunderstanding 101
Heartburn Studies
The Novelette
Troubleshooting the Mithridatised
The Modern Underachiever
Draw in H, 2H, 3H, 4H, 5H, 6H, 7H, 8H & 9H (& Rub)
Footnote Clutter
NSFW
Father K.:
Doubt
Hebrew
The Churchy Batholith
Bird Orthography
To Deflower The Footpath & Ha-Ha
Cottonmouth
Noncomformity
Downloaded Hoodoo
Adah:
Threat
Bayonetting

★

A double kitchen, unventilated.
CAIN: Hive the territories tighter.
ADAH: How do we reign?
CAIN: Through obviousness.
FR. K.: Autonomously.
CAIN: That toot will be your only line, wretch!
[Slays him.]
H.R.H.: Fab. Art thou happy? Mm?
ADAH: No. Th- Thou?
H.R.H.: More than this tic bulb degenerate browbeaten horridly earth-
ward. Or than—
ADAH: Cheat!
H.R.H: Outvoted, underdressed offender, hormone offshoot. *[He teethes.]*
Th- th- th- th- th- the doghood dethronement. Best end—
[End.]

from *The Learned Pig*

53

Gillingham

◇   ◇   ◇

Here the sands and me were sinking.
The house though upright, wore its mourning.
Nothing to lean into save the marcasite gutter

people dumped polished wood furniture into.
Internal walls came down. My father had a room
of his own, red, with a piano and Lenin,

who took up a whole wall. Upstairs I shared
with my sister; my three brothers in another.
We were in this together –

went shrimping from a stairwell on the Medway,
sold flimsy crabs to the cornershop,
were never dry enough when out in the rain.

We'd watched the films. Threat of war, invasion, pirate
capture was sincere. We hid in the Admiral's Gardens,
necessary helicopters above. Played football

or sat reverential in the air raid shelter,
decorated with posters of Garfield and Tom Cruise.
I learned to run, to secure a candle to a plate.

I learned fear has its uses, like when there's a wire fence
to scale and how to steal, the Sunday School
deserved it. I knew the church, with its shallow pool

and congregational glare, had it in for us. I knew
the Government had it in for us (I had seen my mother cry).
I knew the Government had it in for us.

I had seen my mother cry and walk out of the house.
I tried 'nougat', I tried 'mango'.
I told my mother she couldn't be my mother

as she had black hair; I had blonde.
I knew life would be impossible without her.
I knew about Thatcher, about being 'in The Red'

and what mattered to Baptists and I had danced, alone,
to all of *True Blue* by Madonna in the kitchen.
I held stick insects and locusts and an old man's penis.

The hospital appointments (I could not hear)
set me apart.
As did seeing the old man ejaculate.

He had Imperial Leather soap and a panic bell
I 'must not to pull'.
I did not know about this.

My brothers and sister and mother
and father I loved, though sometimes with reserve.
Best of all was being in the same car,

the seats folded down, travelling north
or to Minis Bay with a carnival wind,
night-time or lunch with the car doors closed.

One winter the snow was storybook.
We took bin liners to sledge in and our winter clothes
were ruined. I knew the word 'saturated'.

I never expected my dad to be there,
though we marched together. I sought
to cultivate fervour,

for that was how love might be won.
He bought me a violin without my ever asking.

from the *Morning Star*

Sometimes I think the world is just a vast breeding ground for mosquitoes

from 'House for the Study of Water'

◊   ◊   ◊

Dear Max. The stars grow
paler. The sun is rising with
grace and power. I lie here in
my shirt being tried (repeatedly)
by a council of mosquitoes who
find me sorrowful and stupid
and ordinary and rather dull
and worst of all, *his tastes are
vulgar and he writes like a dog.*
But am I an animal? *A dog can't
write . . . Exactly!* In the afternoon
heat I sit with my feet down look-
ing out of the window. What's so
awful about me is not my envy
or my competitiveness or my
cruelty. What's worse is this dog-
like devotion. How sad I look,
sitting here. About whom? About
what? Sometimes when I close
my eyes I imagine *you're* here
watching me. I can't explain it
but I've this bizarre notion that
you might come and carry me
(*like a dog . . . Exactly! Exactly!*)
out of this house, this life, this
world.

from *tender*

Genit—

◇ ◇ ◇

across an empty sea. Arising from my lounger

I could not remember whether I had my vagina on.
Round the saltwater pool undergraduates Yes to sexy
No to desperate. I had picked up their way with vowels
and was making up for it with inimitable consonants.
What I saw leave the hollow of my open hand, wobble
as if played from a speaker through palm trees' blue
shade several windows deep was what a lepidopterist
would recognise as an image in lieu of a real moth.

Bodies have no such exchange Balloons to include me
inside it, from across the water. Spray from each dive

sharpens skin to a point. Pop. The frame Between her
thighs, moths span on their splintered golden wings
while the hot mind caught Plastic acquires a pet name.
Waking reported war, church bells on Audio inaudible
at ear height. All my blood in a pile. Reconnected me
with Latisha from English and a used phrase, 'the number
of things it is possible to think all at once.' The price of

The translation has more moths than the original.
Where clothes end, in lieu of the people themselves
People themselves. Each undergraduate strains to

be more like the others than the others. Stealth's
angles make an obvious plane. One wants to find out
why the lover is not located in the body of the lover.
On a long wooden pier keen automatic men looked
to the ends of their lines six nights of the summer week.
They sensed extension in all directions but knew only

the difficulty of extension. More afraid of meaning
more than I mean, I stay awake through the fun.
Casting off rain, the Wake from committing rape
to find ourselves through commitment. Drawn from

suggestions the environment made, her large wet kisses,
whether I wanted to be included in her large wet kisses.
The bacterium alive on damp leaves of *The Game* lends
substance to the dimension I could not get hold of
between the gym and the gym on the gym TV.

See. Buried by clean linen. Sex is pea. We have sex
on top of Our voices mean more than we mean.
Moth-phobic translator does a book with a moth motif,
spends three years with the question Those fuckers: do we
want to have them or to be them? The object of desire,

whether clothed as teacup or cherub, is also an objection.
A splinter in the leaves. Sunbathing woman becomes aware
of a hair clot shuddering between pimpled white slats
of an overspill slurp and sets and dives to feel the shaved

Fruit sells. It keeps summer inside, like a forecast
App for 'the number of things it is possible to think
all at once' decorates the urge, catching up with
To go at it quickly and hard, a sex-within-sex,
flight which is also reeling in. The water stung
her nose. A tent collapsed with us enormous inside

The pregnant woman shows us where in us
A replacement cherry skin. I can't tell you how
much of what I know is the inability to turn into

You, splintered like the one true cross in the body
of the hedgehog, for whom we put out milk and
Tyres shredded. Whether your moths are more real
or more cultured, I remember dry wings on water
inflating and popped by an Ext. Daytime. Wet
skin soliciting sun. The original author who was
merely fascinated. The late, great European poets

and a chalk outline where No punch-line here. Say it
With American genitalia, I knew desire setting

in the shape of a gelatinous missile. Blindly erect,
a blunt growl, a perfectly squeaking door. Requiring
sex once more to set sex right. And this while it
happened. Everything's parts To spread everywhere
copy text with own emotion. Latisha pumped
my fingers with gas. Information does not resist fantasies
of weapons inspectors but affords them cool air
abundantly in the desert. Another, poorer, nation

loaded with images the shaft where experience collapsed.

Then it seemed suddenly possible to divide time into moments,
        or,
in fact, more accurately, for thinking to be so divided; an
        awareness,
then, I should say, that immediately following the present focus of
        attention,
which itself was, by virtue of that attention, smudged, resulting
in a discernible slowing and the creation, therefore, of space
        around
the present moment, where the attention placed on it exceeded
what it could be attentive to, so the present moment began to slip
        away

– we were translating 'passionate' into the original text.
Latisha said she cleaned her teeth with pubic hair –

before the anticipated moment had arrived, so a third moment,
brought into being by attention itself – as if it was censorship.
A folder A fig leaf placed over the photograph of the enemy
naked on the desktop. A window appears and through it Better.
So-called iceberg properties. If only the petals glued back on.
The water closed. The knickers climbed for the hand to disturb

for a first time. I sprinkled coins into the open coffin
as if they were money. White slats, slurping overspill, gold
sliding down the face. The instinct hooked in the mouth

in which Adam's mouth spoke, against 'death', without
quotation marks, in my mouth furious with thanks.
I meant to say the one great question is: to whom or what
should I give my thanks? They automatically undress again.
Parts which sin grow plastic and large, more real and yet further

Balloon trapped in a moth's heart. Each eager stroke reduces
likelihood of sky, straining to extend below the waterline.
We are not one another. With that prefatory statement each,
they came. A dense blob of paint thinned with clear water.

Pale streaks Home to species invisible to the Passion pulled
away from me like an artificial fly. After he had been done
he noticed her steadying hand on the rubber travels ever so
slightly quicker than the escalator itself. View completed

by a competing view, even as the sum of the two views wants
completion, even as many affluent homes acquire new rooms
beneath to stay on top of Dragged the water into me Instead,
the city shouts up to the bedroom window, 'We can't hear you.
We really have no idea what you are doing up there together.'

Foundation had collected in the throat, too shy to bring it up.
For that gift of extension into someone else was received
without growth or erosion. When asked if she was sexy

or desperate it appeared that she had no place in language.
Afterwards the objection became the lover. To undress,
to sleep with, in lieu of the People themselves are never
enough. Or too much. The pool itself drains me. Balloons
become cushions, the source becomes pale streaks of blue
Dribble. So many thoughts become one thought, and rather than

a thought they divided themselves into, it was a thought
divided by them. Catching You has the outside

arranged so that its inside is the landscape behind
the portrait. To replace childhood's broken chintz,
0.1% APR. For the price of light, a moth. State
the word to bring about agreement to use the word.
Sex is performed to make sex possible. Bodies rise
to meet bodies. Each line cast into the night sea
straightened with the same imagined flight. Each took in

the same weightless attention and offered the same slack.

Having closed in on death, the men hurl plaice.
The moth meant other things and had no equivalent.
The taut lounger sodden with punctured shade.
With the distance fucked out of one another, they
returned from the coffin to The frame, splashed,
took on the colour of Their heads returned to
their heads. But he finished himself off every time
he sat down to One more equivalent: where I came

From *The White Review*

The Word

◇ ◇ ◇

I couldn't tell you now what possessed me
to shut summer out and stay in my room.
Or at least attempt to. In bed mostly.
It's my dad, standing in the door frame
not entering – but pausing to shape advice
that keeps coming back. 'Whatever is matter,

must *enjoy the life*.' He pronounced this twice.
And me, I heard wrongness in putting a *the*

before *life*. In two minds. Ashamed. Aware.
That I knew better, though was stuck inside
while the sun was out. That I'm native here.
In a halfway house. Like that sticking word.
That definite article, half right, half
wrong, still present between *enjoy* and *life*.

from *The Poetry Review*

girl vs. sincerity

◇　◇　◇

the elderly man is baffled
by the 'Toast Station' for commuters
amid carnage of almond butter and seeded bloomer
he has reduced his muffin to rubble
all is crust and I want to hold him
because of the news
or the daisycutters which aren't apprentice stylists
or things for your pubes
there goes Marinetti

with words, and bombs

★

went howling mad on Lupus Street
on a calm day, with lady grey by the curb
I diagnose the sky with SAD
its stormlets slip through the sun

★

my six-year-old sister says the worry dolls don't work
and their arms are broken
my inner misogynist says don't worry doll and thinks
of that Irvine Welsh story where he fucks a Thalidomide babe
turned on by her lack of arms cos she can't push him away

instead I gulp sick and tell her they never had arms
and: 'keep trying'

★

by day I compile manifestos
and resolve to gouge out my eyes
because they won't stop policing
all the women-bodies

★

dogshit after rain
sometimes smells ok

from *clinic*

i am very precious

◊　◊　◊

I see all the black marks on the page, the lines
hallucinations falling off the edge of the world – my tongue
we haven't talked about desperation,
yet you tell me about pornography, girls with death wishes
attached to their libidos, little warm arrows
aligned to their supple bodies, inside where the parental hole gapes;
do you understand that when the day breaks
semen in the body turning over like a silk belt, slashing
the way the poetry aches like it does when fantasies
abate and leave beds turning over like guillotined heads
and my eyesight's killing the words as they fall
into the blinking retinas and all the images burned inside
tearing the cloth on your body with wide-eyed
longing. My darling, you write, my darling, my love
reach into the glove compartment and pass me my map,
and my scissors to snip your underwear, to snip at your heart,
little buckles undone to reveal the muscle torn
and purple and ermine and the little black leather
buckles. When I used to wear my fuck-me boots and walk
the streets at night I could feel men looking at my melancholy curves
I felt hot and I wanted to call home and say my death
was not only imminent but simply a scar that never healed –
crying in my sleep, my chest heaving and my body fastened
to every shape ever thrown in the bed in June
when Nature told me to no longer be pregnant. I'm a big girl
I said. Roomy in the hips like Buffalo Bill's victims
in *Silence of the Lambs*. I oil my skin
so the desire will slip off me and onto the floor and crawl
around and get carpet burns and I will glow
like a cigarette burn on the arm of the whitest smack-head
in town, I will glow like the face of the girl who loves him and is
　　willing

to watch him die out, slowly, and with no flames to fan.
I was that girl. I made him listen to a song I loved
and he cried like he'd never cried in his life that this girl with cuts
on her skin would have liked to hold him, crawl into his
psychiatric ward bed and breathe all over his damp, white shoulders.
Some people don't actually want to be wanted.
Some people actually want to be harmed. I used to fantasise
about being annihilated. About being so completely overwhelmed
the dark would rush in on me and fill me up inside
hard like whiplash in the back of a Ford Estate; stop my heart
dead on contact with the heart, the thudding heart. Wanting to be
        loved is not the same
as wanting to be fucked is not the same as wanting to come last
is not the same as wanting to be married. Not wanting to be married.
Wanting not to heal up inside and the tears
ruby, glowing tears in the skin just sting in the morning
and are easy to cover up. I told you last night about the baby
that died, you told me not to talk about it and I was glad
you were so on my side that talking about dead babies was bad.
Dead babies. I tried to explain how they don't stay with you long,
and you told me how your sister went in the wrong grave –
I'm gonna have to pace myself; that's what men tell me
they have to do when they're with a woman;
it's easy to get consumed and the main thing is to hold out.
Death has come out of me, before love has wound its way
to my thigh. The things I have lost fill my toy-museum heart
and when you take me all the dolls get wound up and the bears
start barking. Hand-jobs just don't do it for me, I'm sorry –
maybe if I really like you, you can tell me about it. I like to hang on the
        line
and when the feeling coos in my mouth for an outlet
and I want the voice of someone with a heart that knows about hearts
that know about hearts that know and can give me their thumb
to suck and say you can't handle the way I want you;
when I don't know if I can; and I only do it with men
with really clean hands. When I am rubbing my heart against
the sofa like a sexed-up cat, rubbing up against the bedclothes,
rubbing up against the fictional thighs of Northern Goddesses
pull me in all directions. I want to be told.
Tell me. My sense of abandon is an alcoholic, and you're
co-dependent. In the night I dream of Adolf and the fictional
loins of Northern Gods and the vacant lane to the abattoir
where the boys hang out looking for pussy

at five a.m. when the girls come on their shift in their shitty jeans.
I want to hang on the line and get all torn up.
I want to stare at women in shops when they're not even that attractive
just look *expensive*. And the perfume they wear isn't so tempting
but it covers the sex they had hours before and how they
don't want to smell of it anymore. Being ravaged is like
someone howling your name so it vibrates in
the *caves of your sex*. You want to ravage me don't you
don't you want to ravage me. You want to ravage me so much
you don't even know where you'd start, you haven't
figured that out, or maybe when you're alone and no-one is there
the plan remains the same. Start from the top and work your way
      down.
This is no longer the poem I expected.
Being rejected has always got me hot – being turned down,
being wanted and turned down for no real reason, being desired
and being tormented, and not having what I want
gets the blood flowing to my knickers and when I'm really wet
I'm so wet I can't do nothing about it and it hurts.
I can tell you this because nothing fazes you about me,
even my fucking regular heartbeat. In the night
I lie like a little snail stuck to the edge of a wall and get really moist.
I don't want to do it anymore. I'd like simply to talk
about other poetic pursuits, like addictions, and walking at dusk
and making soup. Hounds call after me where I run with shaved legs
to come back and make coffee. Just try something simple and easy
and do nothing with my mouth. My red and open mouth,
my wet and pink and closed mouth, swallowing
my ordinary mouth with wet lips opening, my tongue –
fuck off, you said. I'm a big girl. I know you watch porn
and all the hairless girls with hopeless drug addictions lick each other
like stage-struck puppies. They don't mean it, you know that.
It's not like that when I get my tongue around someone;
it barely lasts five minutes most of the time, always has.
I don't like it to go on for a long time. My scars itch and I get so wet
I get drowned. I've had boyfriends who've tried to get me
to watch porn with them but it's the lack of perceived sensation,
their bodies just seem numb, like if they were enjoying it they'd
just fucking melt. Melt into the screen, with their dumb, lame, orange
skin and a sound like you're supposed to make when a climax comes
so slow and steady you're silk, the heart turning over
like a silk belt; the little black buckles of the heart snapping
in turn. I don't want to take my clothes off for anyone; want to

sleep with my t-shirt on and wake in a fever, my legs closed
and my hands under my pillow. These things eat me up inside.
I want to be eaten up inside. I want to abstain.
I want to be hungry. I want to hunger for nothing want
annihilation in a pile on the floor, want annihilation to creep
along the floor to my heels, push its head between my legs and seep
into my skin. All the things I have done before
are yesterday's sins. Skinny dipping in the reservoir. Dressing up.
You've got to hide the mirror, you've got to hide
the mirror. You can't handle me, and I'll only last sixty seconds.
And I'm gonna brush my hair one hundred times
and wear red satin, and sit at the dresser, and look in the mirror
and in the mirror and in the mirror I saw
a girl, a little younger than me, as vacant as a dream of a house
in which everyone you know goes to live and disappears.
And I saw a girl, so tightly spun it'd take an avalanche
of desire. And I saw a girl so sad the whole sorry affair went by
without celebration. My head is very tired now
for all my thinking about my body, how different parts
of my body feel differently. I don't understand why anyone would go
to a swingers party. Or watch hand-job porn while their partner
wrote poetry. I don't want to see anyone come
but you. I'm gonna brush my hair one hundred times, looking
in the fucking mirror and hope to god I don't
only last sixty seconds or maybe just hope that I don't die too soon.
That the leather buckles that fasten my heart to my chest
are kept down, and a silver stream of semen
goes nowhere near my abdomen. I want
everything and more besides. I want the wholeness
of my psychological make-up to stay whole and ripe. I want my
          wholeness
to retain its mystery and I want my breasts to get bigger,
and my ass to get smaller, and my belly to disappear.
Like the orange girls who lick each other's pale nipples,
orange like they've all come from some other land
hairless like they've all come from some other place
where beauty gets defaced just so men can come all over
faces made ugly by insincerity. When you're not sincere
how can you climax. The afterthoughts of all of this are
I'm not worth the heat, sweat or blood pressure. If you had sex
all day with orange fictional Northern Goddesses, you'd not need
to go to the gym. When my boyfriend made me watch porn one time
they did a lot of bouncing. I kind of thought this looked

uncomfortable and strange. I thought if I did that all day I'd get bruised
inside and I imagined their purple, ermine, ruby insides
their uteruses lined with stinging salt. The baby that died
took a small part of my heart. I buried that baby
in the toilet of a downstairs flat, where it was so cold
the window had iced up. I have had to stop.
Blood pours into all of my poems like it floods
the veins around my clitoris when someone says they like my
name. So please do say it again.

from *Prac Crit*

DOROTHY LEHANE

Sombrero galaxy

◊ ◊ ◊

Wild behemoth, replete
with assemblage, leading a reaction
to spiral arms. Neat. Hats–down.
Plethora dansé: *sweet little mystery*.
Galactic four stomach throng
super black hole burning to feed

uncertainty is centrifugal force

since equilibrium is a post–it note:
post hoc propter hoc

sweep the sky, listen to the radio

do you hear the underground emcee
dans le découpage, insipid
relentless hiss, trace the solo dust lane
backlit, red–lit, dancing without legs:
nudie nudie nudie
sweet rhinestone mystery.

from *Tears in the Fence*

Melpomene

◇ ◇ ◇

And he says I have this hardly original
hole inside of me; that I am two things
infinitely: carnal and futile. He's right.
I am a bad wife, a wanting quarry
of witless worry; lank rage, grim schlock,
and stroppy poverty. I am sleazed in
the green of The Land, raining down
her birdsong in blows. The dubby
crush of my keening does his head in.
I sink kisses into screams like pushing
pennies into mud. And he says he is done.
From the wordy murk of my loss come
lanterns and daggers, and I am my country:
mean, gutless and Medieval; a dread
mess of battlements and spoils. He cannot
love me, grieved to my gills and grinding
exile like an axe. He cannot love me,
howling out my mutant blues to no one.
My semi-automatic sobbing wakes
the neighbours. I am sorry. I have tried
to live lightly, to live like *gadje* girls,
to make my mouth an obedient crock
of homage; to keep my swift hands soft
in illiterate peachiness. But I am from
an ugly world, an ugly world with ugly
songs for busking in an underpass. I am
not one of your machine-washable muses,
my face a cotton swab. I cannot come
clean, come cosy, come tame and fond.
His suckling fund of human love destroys
me. I am not good. I am a ferreting girl
who steals from shops, a perfidious febrile

girl who gobs off bridges; a hedging
and fretting girl, one eye on the exit.
I am terrible. I drink myself to a fly-
tipped farrago of falling down. No decorum
in me. My mourning is eloquent strumpetry,
and ruin porn will always be the whole
of my Law. I am sorry. And he says he
cannot love me in my insolent libidiny;
my shrill pandemic ditties: poems bleating
like woebegone ringtones. He cannot love me
in my words, raptures dragged from the slangy
waste of Norn. He says he will have none,
when a poem is a viral fire that spreads my anger
round; a typo-tastic war grave in which I bury
my dead. And he says I am *damaged*. I frisk
the heart for sadness, find it waiting
like a toothache. It is true. Thrice fool girl,
dangled at a day's end, what have I got
besides? There is only this particular fire
in me, this brief biotic craze of light, a halo
like a yellow enzyme: luciferase, fanatical,
and *dragging us down*, he says. He leaves
and slams the door. I breathe again. The TV
leaks a sour myrrh meaning evening. I scuff
my breath on the edges of an empty room.
Here is the moon, poor feme sole,
and the orange stars in their cold swoon.

from *The Poetry Review*

ADAM LOWE

Vada That

◇　◇　◇

Aunt nell the patter flash and gardy loo!
Bijou, she trolls, bold, on lallies
slick as stripes down the Dilly.

She minces past the brandy latch
to vada dolly dish for trade, silly
with oomph and taste to park.

She'll reef you on her vagaries –
should you be so lucky. She plans
to gam a steamer and tip the brandy,

but give her starters and she'll be happy
to give up for the harva. Mais oui,
she's got your number, duckie.

She'll cruise an omi with fabulosa bod,
regard the scotches, the thews, the rod –
charpering a carsey for the trick.

Slick, she bamboozles the ogles
of old Lilly Law. She swishes
through town, 'alf meshigener, and blows

lamors through the oxy at all
the passing trade. She'll sass a drink
of aqua da vida, wallop with vera in claw.

Nellyarda her voche's chant till the nochy
with panache becomes journo, till
the sparkle laus the munge out of guard.

But sharda she's got nada, she aches
for an affaire, and dreams of pogey
through years of nix. The game nanti works

— not for her. She prefers a head
or back slum to the meat rack. Fact is,
she'll end up in the charpering carsey

of Jennifer Justice. What is this
queer ken she's in? Give her an auntie
or a mama. The bones isn't needed just yet.

Though she's a bimbo bit of hard,
she's royal and tart. And girl, you know
vadaing her eek is always bona.

from *Vada Magazine*

Glossary

aunt nell — ear, listen (also: nellyarda) | patter flash — gossip, chat | gardy loo — 'Look out!' |
troll — walk | lallies — legs | The Dilly — Piccadilly, a high street or similar | brandy — bottom
(from Cockney rhyming slang 'brandy and rum') | vada — see, spy, look | dolly — pretty | trade,
trick — a sexual partner | reef — to feel, to grope (especially the bulge or crotch) | harva — anal
sex | omi — man | scotches — legs | thews — thighs, sinews | charpering — finding | vera — gin |
nochy — night | journo — day | laus — chases | munge — darkness | sharda — though | affaire — a
lover, a serious partner | pogey — money | head — bed | back slum — public lavatory | meat
rack — brothel | charpering carsey — police cell | auntie — older gay man, role model | mama —
mentor | the bones — a boyfriend or husband | eek — face | bona — good

CHRIS MCCABE

The Repossessor

◇　◇　◇

sits in the chair where the Chief once sat
his smooth hands leafed in a collapse of polyester
as the dog's eyes milk sleep
– old age heels her to its elbow –
She will die soon The Repossessor says
not looking from the prospectus of viewings in laminate
decking The Avenues of local markets,
he knows by instinct who is dead, divorced, in arrears
– nets & blinds morph shadows for that –
upstairs are young bookmakers, ribbed at the ribs,
signing for careers in leisure & fitness,
The Repossessor already knows the roads where love
will thorn nests in them – the fixed names of streets
where taxis purr for cash – as supermarkets & Polaris
pour change into drunkenness,
The Repossessor knows that the details
of all things named moves us faster upwards
than the new naming of one unlabelled thing,
the dog coughs dust into the fender, deaf in both ears,
blind in one eye, The Repossessor shifts in his seat,
calculates decreases
for the banana wine the Chief over-fermented for years
        maxed to mass volume under outdoor bricks
for the polystyrene spitfires grounded to white pips
                in the waist-length grass
for the outside bath filled with snow for cats
        to tabulate with shadows
for the first boardgame in primary colours
   with no counter to win or lose play cash
for the VHS stillframes of Warner & Disney
   frozen for the hours Walt cracked in his grove of ice
for the stinkbombs brewed from suds & spices

loaded & lodged under siblings' bunks
for the knee cicatrix stitched to diary pages
    as time healed itself to Summer each year.
The Repossessor pulls a black card from his pocket,
pushes it back – *O God*, he says, as the silence
of the dog's bowels startles his concentrates –
The Chief has no need of bricks now –
and the market announces us.

        from *The Wolf*

Kadmea Touch Me

◊ ◊ ◊

I said *Oedipa* she said *what*
I said *Oedipa*

how do you know you're alive she said
pinch me OK

so I did I grabbed the tender bulge of flesh just
inside her arm

the soft deposit of fat that lasts a lifetime I squeezed it as
hard as I

could I squeezed it & squeezed it until my face went red & puffy
& I was

crying *Oedipa* I said *Oedipa don't you know you're alive yet* she just stared
straight ahead with

those big black eyes & I knew then she would never know I knew no one could help
her & I

held her in my arms for a whole night and a whole day *one should search for the truth & not*
exceptional conditions I

said *the truth only exists in exceptional conditions* she said *why don't you touch me*
I said *I'm*

holding you it's not enough she said *how can I know I'm alive unless you*
touch me I

didn't say a word what could I say tell me what could I say so I
grabbed her flesh

again the fatty underhang & I squeezed it & squeezed
it until I

thought my finger and thumb would drop off
she didn't even

blink *I love you Oedipa no you don't*
she said *if*

you really loved me you
would touch me

from *The Rialto*

End Space

◇   ◇   ◇

will write while the light is good   I have been asked to write
    in a room like this   you think of the hiding places first
ecret drawers   dusty chairs behind metal shutters   there is a smell
        of medicine in the air   but I do not look sick   I look great
rom this window I can see   empty hospital beds   lined up against
he sea wall   yellowing pillows   I have been asked to not think too hard
nd if I do want to think   it should be something from this book
he examples   'your childhood pet'   'meadows covered in mist'
    'balls of different sizes in a stadium'   'spring flowers'

oday I went on a walk   my third this week   I found the tennis courts
    the rackets lined up like machine guns   I played a few rounds solo
itting the ball against the wall wasn't that fun   but the sound echoed back
    from the cobweb corners   when I found the pool   it was a mirror
I wanted to swim   but instead I looked down   on the patterned ceiling
    I went outside for the first time   I saw how the branches of the trees
vere held back by wire   to teach them their shape   a new shape   also
here is a church here   on the door there is a sign that reads   'No service'
t is fixed by shoelaces   who is watering my plants at home?   my brain feels dirty

s if it has grown a beard   I want to wake up very early to see how
he day changes   so I could say to someone   'well, it was much nicer earlier'
ut I feel slow   I haven't seen anyone for a while   my bones feel like broken water
    when I stand on the beach   I can see sirens   along the coast held tightly
vith rust   I wonder why   they are there   and then it starts   I think
    of the out of season   holiday camps   that we visited   the wide waters
    remember the way   you held your ice cream cone   your amphitheatre fingers
        I think of how each new building has designs   to stop people
    from jumping off them   steel netting   and impossible ledges

there are people   that spend their lives   seeing men and women
in the flower beds   and garden them   I can't see anyone by the time
I find my room again   standing by the window   a few beds
are still out there   I reach for the book   and read out the prompts
'snow-capped mountain peaks'   'smaller babies'
'a sink filled with water and wine glasses'   'empty white bird houses'

from *Poetry London*

ANDREW MCMILLAN

Ókunna Þér Runna

◇ ◇ ◇

there are dead in countries
who will never know how
little I despised them
I wanted the penblade
not the bootsplatter trenchlife
the night I ran   there was
sky concealing thunder
a white feather of moon

★

the words give heavy page
the words bleed out of me
bullstrong   I like to think
of guns   the sound of rain
Hemingway's forearm thick
as tree root   men are dead
who never wondered what
I thought   or why   or not

★

I am deadheavydrunk
sharpen penblade   moonglint
now think of Hemingway
swallowing a shotgun
now think of bulls   enraged
now think of men who can't
be men without dying
of rain of Thanes of Harr

from *Modern Poetry in Translation*

KATHRYN MARIS

It was discovered that gut bacteria were responsible

◊   ◊   ◊

It was discovered that gut bacteria were responsible
for human dreams. Each bacterium was entitled to pay
a fee in the form of mitochondrial energy to purchase
a 'dream token' to be dropped into a Potential Well. These
'tokens' were converted to synaptic prompts and transported
to the human brain in no particular order. So a 'token' for a
'baseball dream' deposited in the well when the human host
was aged 8 might only be used by the brain when the host
was 44, and this dream that might have been pleasant for an
8-year-old could instead emerge as a nightmare for a woman
on the brink of menopause who might worry about her
appearance in a baseball uniform, or who no longer recalled
how to hold a baseball glove and catch a ball in the field.

from *Granta*

Silence, Singing

◇　◇　◇

These are the words I was given.

> Be a good daughter.
> Lead a good life.
> Find a good husband.
> Be a good wife.

It was the first poem anyone had ever written for me: my grandmother inscribed it in my bat-mitzvah present, an Artscroll machzor, the prayer book for the High Holydays.

★

In my matching Artscroll *siddur*, I could have found this short prayer said daily: 'Blessed are you, Lord our God, Ruler of the Universe, who has not made me a woman.'

Not that I would have been in synagogue for weekday morning prayers: as a woman, my presence couldn't count towards *minyan*, the quorum for prayer, and I couldn't wear *tefillin*, the phylactery that literally ties God's word to the skin.

★

Now I have escaped the binds of a 'life' chiming only with 'wife', what I see in the inscription is, paradoxically, how I learned to escape: the power-fully profane act of handwriting, on a holy book, a prayer of your own.

★

I had precedent.

Mary Sidney Herbert, Countess of Pembroke, is one of the earliest known female poets in English, and one of the first women to translate sacred texts into the vernacular. After the death of her brother, Sir Philip Sidney, she continued his work on a metrical translation of the Book of Psalms, including Psalm 130, the famous 'De profundis clamavi'.

Translation is a kind of mutation. Like Mystique, Mary Sidney slips into the skins of a series of men. Not only her brother, but also other English psalms translators: Thomas Wyatt, George Gascoigne, Thomas Sternhold and William Whittingham.

And behind them, King David, legendary lover/fighter, conqueror poet, to whose bloodied hand and honeyed tongue the Psalms are attributed.

With his tongue in her mouth, Mary Sidney is seeking her own solution: at once poem and prayer.

★

The opening of her translation of 130 sets out the stakes:
> From depth of greif
>> Where droun'd I ly,
> Lord for releife
>> To Thee I cry:
> my ernest, vehment, cryeng, prayeng,
> graunt quick, attentive, heering, waighing.

★

As Anne Carson argues in her essay 'The Gender of Sound', no-one likes to hear a woman's 'vehment, cryeng' – which is often how women's writing is heard. Confessional, over-emotional, nonsensical, hysterical. But Mary Sidney insists that 'cryeng' is also 'prayeng', a protestation of the individual relationship with God – or, in a secular sense, the right to speak and be heard.

If the life others have prayed for you is 'wife', how can you demand that right?

★

Perhaps the depths – *mima'amakin* in Hebrew – create their own language. What cannot be articulated invents, in its urgency, new articulation. Perhaps you need that new language because you're at the limits of where good behaviour can take you: 'greif', or rage, or desire, or their meeting point.

'De profundis' was the title posthumously given to Oscar Wilde's famous letter from prison, one it shares with dozens of poems in the European canon.

★

Elizabeth Barrett Browning, another precedent for squaring the circle of being a (good) girl and being a poet, wrote a 'De Profundis' after the death of her husband. In it, she says: 'I knock and cry, – Undone, undone!'

Here we are at the edge of language: 'undone', a word that undoes itself. It speaks its unspeakability. It dares to unlace the corset of good behaviour.

★

Thomas Wyatt also used Psalm 130 to comment on the limits of good behaviour. It's likely he translated it between his arrest on allegations of adultery with Anne Boleyn in 1536 and his death in 1542.

He translated it as part of the sequence known as the Penitential Psalms, supposedly written by David after he had his lover Bathsheba's husband murdered. Murder (not to mention both sexual and military conquest) is the murky depth from which David prays.

Yet David's account of his seduction of Bathsheba – like his defeat of Goliath the Palestinian, and subsequent conquest of Palestine – is still told, and heard, as a boast, rather than penitence.

★

Wyatt opens Psalm 130:
> From depth of synne, & from depe dispayre
> Fro depth of deeth, fro depth of hart's sorowe
> Fro this depe caue, of darkenes, depe repayre
> The haue I called (O Lorde) to be my borowe

★

Wyatt calls on God 'to be [his] borowe' – a convenient rhyme for sorrow, but one that implies a curious relationship between the speaker and his listener.

Mary Sidney seeks 'quick, attentive, heering, weighing'. Using the present participle, Gertrude Stein's favourite part of speech, she implies reciprocity. Wyatt, though, is cutting a deal.

The OED cites his line for the word's obsolete definition as a noun: 'borrow, of persons: A surety, hostage; bail, deliverer from prison'. He's looking for God to bail him out.

★

Borrow is first found as a noun in the Laws of Aethelred in 1000. The medieval poets Rolle and Langland use it with the spelling 'borgh[e]' to mean a pledge or loan. It derives from the Old German *berg-an*: to protect, shelter, to shut in for protection. Berg-an leaves its trace in the words borough, burgher, bourgeois, and Borgen; also burrow, bury, and burial.

The walls that keep us safe will also wall us in.

Not Wyatt, though. Even in prison, he knows he's good for a loan from the God zone. In the depths of grief, he turns glibly to the language of power, of money and law. Status: quo.

★

I was brought up to believe that my body was borrowed from (in ascending order) husband, father and God; rights in it passed directly from the last to the latter to the first. There were no words I could own, or in which to own myself.

★

A girl stands at the edge of an armed camp, at the edge of the sea. Usually turbulent, they have both fallen still. A suspended hush. Like Bathsheba's, her body is the pivot of a war, subject of a king's law. It is a borrow.

One story says that before she was born, her father the king offered a god the most beautiful thing he saw that year. Another source says the god demanded a sacrifice before a king could go to war against his Eastern neighbours.

86

Most sources say nothing at all. About her, Iphigenia.

The Furies' judgement on her brother's revenge for her mother's vengeance for her murder at her father's hands will become, in Aeschylus' account, the foundation of the Athenian state, the buried secret at the heart of law.

She is the borgh[e], berg-an, the invisible security on which our myth of democracy stands.

★

Euripides wrote two plays about Iphigenia. They are our main source for her story, and he told it backwards: in the first play, *Iphigenia among the Taurians*, she is alive and the war is over. The god that wanted her dead has saved her.

Artemis 'translates' her from under her father's knife, substituting a deer. A priestess of a death cult in Tauris, Iphigenia cures and saves her vengeance-maddened brother so they can return to Athens – and the Furies, who will rule her murder insufficient cause for her mother's revenge.

★

The sacrifice happens offstage in the second play, *Iphigenia at Aulis*, Euripides' final – and bleakest – work. The limits of his language.

The only evidence here for the Artemis translation is a messenger's speech, or rather a fragment from it cited in an obscure grammar book, not present in any other surviving text of the play. Some critics argue Euripides didn't finish it before he died. Couldn't.

There are no facts on the ground; the incompossible versions are entangled with the untanglable knot of Iphigenia's sacrifice and its necessity. If she dies, then vengeance, then law. If she is saved, then vengeance, then law.

★

After all the words for kill, there is a silence. In the silence, singing. 'Vehment, cryeng' that men do not want to hear.

In *Agamemnon*, Aeschylus has the Watchman tell the Chorus that Iphigenia tried to sing when she was brought to the altar. He says that she had sung prayers at her father's table. Who knows, says the Watchman, what curse she would have called down had they not gagged her.

From the depths, she cries out. Undone, undone.

★

The cry and the knife: we know which cuts the silence.

A history in which Iphigenia is allowed to sing – in which her song changes her ending – is not the history we live in. And yet (listen) it is.

★

There is no unwriting Iphigenia's death. But there is writing it: borrowing it, not to shore up the security of the status quo, but to graffiti the walls. Not to uphold the law, but to break it.

We are listening – 'quick, attentive, heering, waighing' – at the limits of hearing, between his lines, for her song. Being undone, she (in silence) sings.

from *The Wolf*

KIM MOORE

The Knowing

◇　◇　◇

The story goes that the light slipped past/and entered the
room like a shout/he stood over me/ a woodcutter entered
the forest/and the trees began to warn each other/it was
July or maybe June/the knowing settled at my throat/a
clever raven/it never left/does not believe in trees or
flying/the light slipping past/it is sometimes painful/to have
a knowing at your throat/that clever raven/but better than
the alternative/something small and bruised/the raven
knows most things/it remembers nothing/this is really
about the trees/which saw it all.

from *Poem*

The Dilemma of al-Kamali

◊ ◊ ◊

In every muscle there is a suppressed howl
And like no other scream is the scream of a knockdown
It is the despair of fear and timidity
Inside the boxing ring
Hands are now truncheons
They know no mercy

Is the arena like a balance
The size, the height, are of no importance?
But scales themselves are a misleading measure
The two pans are never equal even when they appear so
How can a kilo of dust equal a kilo of blood?
Look at it
Look at it
A king-size statue on top of the court-building
A statue of cool, limestone sobriety
The sword is in the right hand
The scales of justice in the other
Reassuring of course but look at it again
Visual consolation no more
Since when is damage redeemed by punishment
Playing on words
Maybe just like tranquillisers
A temporary truce between pain and screams
The damage could last for ever

But what has this to do with Mr Kamali!
Have I lost the knack of versifying
Why should I start with a tedious preface
Only in begging should there be a stutter
Only in a new love should there be hesitation

Again what have the scales to do with Mr Kamali?
Or indeed why has boxing cropped up from nowhere?
We were not fighting
There is no ring after all
At least none that anyone could see

It is true he is some inches taller than me
His chest is high like a sportsman
On the scales or indeed in the ring
Size, height or width can hardly matter
Let him show off then and who cares
He was a minister
Used to having a hotline to the president
And cracking dirty jokes with him
So what! I have my own dignity that should be kept intact
Yes, to the bitter end

It is true we were not in a ring
At least none that anyone could see

Oddly, the first bout began on the train

We sat opposite each other
His cheeks were rigidly tense and getting darker
Like burnt meat
His high chest was gasping for air
Aquatic animal stranded on dry land
Writhing
As if suffering from a stone in his bladder
(It was taken out by a surgical operation
It had the shape of a heart
His wife made a hole in it and wore it as a necklace)

The train moved slowly but with sure puffs
The buildings on both sides also moved like rivers
Cold wind sneaked up the trousers
First he drew back his head
In the way of a tyrant who does not want to listen

Some inches taller than me
His chest is a hand-span wider than mine
So what I said to myself
I will never throw in the towel

Even if he wears a lion's mane
I put my dignity in one pan
Let him put all his offices and rhymed verses in the other

I was waiting cautiously for his first move

He looked at the meadows full-face
They were neatly lined as if by a ruler and compass
Freshly green as far as one can see
Spotted with cattle and tractors and larks

All of a sudden a sigh burst out
That could blow out ten candles at once

Better be silent he said in a veiled voice
Walls have ears hinting at the authorities
And the patch he added is smaller than the rip*
His face is getting darker still
A smoke of conspiracy clouded his eyes
Has he a coup up his sleeve?

– Secrets are amassed on the scales
They are heavier than all weights and measures –

The train drives on through the cutting icy winds

And passes small cities without reducing its speed

Trains make faces yet paler
And mouths drier
And skins stickier
And bladders heavier

He bit the sandwich with a wry face
Looked at it with disgust and threw it out of the window
It flew away in the air with his teeth-marks

My fortresses were crumbling
And swollen was the silence between us
A lump of pain not unlike a fish bone stuck in my throat
The silence getting bigger and more aggressive
Like a suppressed roar in a muscle

He looked at a far-away hut in the meadow
By itself it was standing
As if germinated by force of nature
And with the voice of a ewe having an abortion
Mr Kamali ruefully said
I wish I could shut myself from the world in that hut

What! it is really welling up
Yes it's welling up
It is a real tear
He looked at me then the tear fell down
I heard him sobbing like a little boy

Some years later no more than the five fingers on one hand
It was rumoured that sorrow had killed him
Or was it a heart attack
At his funeral no escort to his final resting place
Others say he was torn to pieces inside prison
Like the flag of a hostile state.

translated by the author; edited by David Andrew

from *Long Poem Magazine*

*An Iraqi slang proverb which means the situation is hopeless or impossible

Artificially Arranged Scenes

after the films of George Méliès

◊   ◊   ◊

Whatever one wants in his world
is what it seems: legs, arms,
an undulating seductress
UT UT RE SI UT
whatever.

Takes off his own head six times
and throws them onto telegraph wires
where they remain familiar with the sea
in an elegant second empire drawing room.

The wolf, being somewhat tied and shut up
in a collection of prolonged standing-on-legs scenes,
while the chorus in pink satin cutaway coats
boil the old lady in her own scullery copper not even

                                              trapdoors thought of,
creeps behind falling snow.

Lanterns dissolve and disembark from a pleasure boat.
Treads on hose. A veritable sledgehammer chez Robert.
And men into women leads to another mysterious box.
Christ, in pumps, on water, takes a Madeleine Bastille omnibus
but before long becomes tired of the Salvation Army and women
forced into prostitution by the tropical conditions only yards from his body.

Likewise a real goat eating hay in 1832
separates the Davenport Brothers,
takes the bags of gold and uses bellows
to inflate his own vigorous rendition of the, then popular, cake walk
as a funnel, also in reverse, a wing
ending in the valley of Chamonix

chugs through an obviously fake mountain scene
bearing the glass slippers in their cabinet.

from *PN Review*

Thank You for Swallowing My Cum

◇ ◇ ◇

I tell cats on the street, 'Hey kitty, she swallowed my cum!'
I told the shy Indian woman in the corner shop, 'Do not be afraid,
for she swallowed my cum!' I even told my mum but she
burned her elbow on the frying pan, and then showed me
a pile of depressing bank statements as my dad blew a perfect
ring of smoke that broke like the ghost of a cheap wedding
band above the empty fruit bowl. While pissing into the sea
on a beautiful day in Barmouth last week, I cupped
my hands around my stoned smile and yelled, 'Hey sunset,
she swallowed my cum!' but it shrugged between misty hills
as the tide rolled over my shoes and my ex-wife hates me.
Or she sometimes hates me. And she never swallowed my cum.
What am I doing? Where am I going? Are you okay?
Can I get you anything? I won't swallow your cum
but I could make you a sandwich. I should probably
send her a message, make sure it's cool to share this
poem. I don't want to make her feel awkward;
awkward that I saw myself clean in her company, my blood
baptismal water; awkward that I saw myself happily dying
as her fingers scribbled sad stories onto my pale chest;
awkward that I tell cats, and nervous Indian women,
and my stressed parents, and amazing, horrible,
gore-porn sunsets that *Oh wow!* when she swallowed
my cum I forgot how dead I am because when I'm living
inside her mouth I don't even need to breathe . . .

from *B O DY*

apples are ¼ air

◊　◊　◊

my husband, the botanist, he dreams green. if you dropped an apple
into the ocean, imagine, it could wash up on an island with nocturnal trees.

the particular way branches branch resemble the pathways through
the heart. these are the things he says in the empty space before sleep.

how tedious to be a man; so perpetually unchallenged. he is making
his own kind of language only the plants comprehend. i paint flowers

in miniature. he tells me this is theft, a liberty and not only that –
preservation, which is contrary to nature. i find joy only in the shrinking.

like a strawberry, he presents his pips on the outside. they are so numerous.
at night the shadows of his hands move like leaves on the walls.

he is a man made up of dark corridors, but he isn't a man at all. you can't
tell me a carnivorous plant doesn't have a brain, a brain and therefore a heart.

perhaps now i am talking about myself. in his greenhouse he is so far away
like a man underwater, a man in a block of ice. when i dream, his mouth

becomes a pea-sized hole and i press the tip of my little finger to it.
i eat him whole. in the immaculate garden the sunflowers rotate with the sun.

from *For Every Year*

HOLLY PESTER

The man from Okay

from 'Jokes That Don't Translate'

◇   ◇   ◇

'how do you like it here?'
they asked him all wet
animal bites
dust eye l
ashes
trampoline covers
as coats
'We've come from the worst hit spot'
really staring as he fixed
them drinks
It's OK 'OK? We were hoping for more
       We've travelled such a way and we're hungry l
             ook at our cattle we're all present tense
     blistering tired disqualified deforged get it alien-like
                   so tired'
OK put it
this way when I came here I had nothing
no language, no clothes my body was limp
they took me
in here fed me here (points to neck and tum) made me
clothes here (points to legs) spoke
to me in Okay sang to me in Okay
danced at me to Okay vouched for me swabbed me
propagated my value oracled my speed & fate and the speed
of my fate (strokes hair) documented it all in Okay
'OK OK how long have you been here?'
I
was
born
here

from *The White Review*

Guess what?

◇ ◇ ◇

From the get-go, we went along with the whopping scam. The whole planet looked like food, and all its muddy creatures our handy/cosmic pizza. We ate hungrily, because eating resembles hunting and hunting resembles love, and we just loved the heat-up-wipe-clean induction hob. We were hell-bent on love. Or our shoddy but realistic guesstimate.

Sex, sex, sex was reliable. Walking along corridors, filling holes with plaster, Bankers Automated Clearance Services, this was sex. Restocking our mouths was sex. Stapling documents was sex. Automated weaponry was sex. Locking and unlocking doors was sex. A particularly satisfying variant involved long-distance chat with no physical contact.

Who am I trying to kid? Excuse me while I peel my banana.

But we did have a trick up our sleeves. Putting it all down to remote control, piloted from thousands of miles away, we could shrug off common feelings like the common cold. We could pump iron.

I'll simply die if I don't.

Duct tape, crude oils, minerals + multi-vits! Anxiety came as standard, or was it anticipation or a frisson of isolation? Quite apart from being indoors, mainly, quite apart from checking the forecast, quite apart from managing the mailbox, we had the wave of the future rushing under our weakening thighs. We spent years pressed to the chest of boredom/waiting, then kerpoW!   a crematorium.

Motion is exhausting. It's a gutsy thing to keep feeling the world's movements.

And that's not really the problem anyway. There was something in the brushwork of FuckYeahNails! that reminded us of the brutal interfaces.

Leopard-print lacquer was revised repeatedly. Women in face-masks attended to our chipped outer-layers. O THANX! we verbalised, because prevention of flaking was tantamount to love-making.

Do you l.o.v.e the sound of trembling in late September?

And then the handle came off my bicycle, right there in my hand, all slithery! Down I went, nosing tarmac, about-to-snuff-it, alone with a road-sign. !But what'll happen to the wet kiss never slapped on his hot lips? !I hadn't been meaning to go on about the sliminess of our situation! !How many handbags I loved and lost! !Don't dead bodies belong to others? Slouched like a bleeding ulcer on a thirsty highway, I saw larvae collecting around the pre-rotten innards. I saw my physical make-up, proportions balanced like an aerated chocolate bar with mint polyps. It wasn't easy to breathe, as usual.

Then I survived. But I hate all that BS. Language is like teeth, which, before we let language appear, were for murdering or caressing. They too have celebrations and die.

A dentist weeps for the rubble scratching our molars.

That's why we get so behind, the daily mega clean-up. Water, thank god, screams like brainwaves and, when it can manage it, floods a person's surfaces with no traces.

Then there's the other side of the argument. Our underpants are shrinking, partly because we're in them too deep, like the contracting continents. After the saturation and the clingy fabrics, wow the circulation bubbles like butter! And melts away.

from *Poetry London*

Apples, Cherries, Apricots & Other Fruits in a Basket, with Pears, Plums, Robins, a Woodpecker, a Parrot, & a Monkey Eating Nuts on a Table

after Clara Peeters

◊   ◊   ◊

I can't stay angry at my little capuchin even though I was looking
    forward to those walnuts
which he holds in his wonderfully long fingers like an anatomist giving
    a lecture on the brain,
before nibbling at the edges as if he was some sort of metaphor for some
    sort of neurological disease.

I know that I cannot trust my little capuchin around fresh fruit: what he
    doesn't eat he smears on the walls
in a fragrant impasto. At first I thought to indulge these creations but
    the black crusts of flies (his only patrons)
were more than I could tolerate. I tried to make him stop & he crushed
    a nectarine into my face.

Whenever my little capuchin looks up at me with those big,
    paperweight eyes, I find reserves
of forgiveness that I never knew existed; suddenly I don't mind so
    much about the broken plates, the shredded
tapestries, the piss-stains on the sofa, the nutty grenades of shit he
    throws to welcome visitors.

He knows that quivering his little capuchin chin & shaking his tail is
      enough to make me turn the other
cheek to the bodies of robins, woodpeckers, parrots, & other birds
      which are littered around his haunches
like the shells of those walnuts which he holds in his wonderfully long
      fingers like a puppeteer.

from *The Poetry Review*

Preferences

◇　◇　◇

People say olives are best served on ice, but I like them room tempera-
ture, in brine, unless it's warm enough to eat outside. I begin in the top
left corner and proceed from left to right, pretty much in the way you'd
imagine. I prefer watercolours of sportscars to an oil painting of dead
people hunting. I include two luminous figures and a huge, black, church-
like interior. I support the early work that supports an alternative reading.
A figure of eight in the acres of parking. I'm not in favour of towns that
bow down to their cemeteries. I sought my revenge in proxy realities.
A nice panic attack in the midwinter market. My picture used to hang
here, but I filled it in with block colour. This is the sixth reproduction. In
practice it's costly, but it costs more than I spent. The moment I'm after
is when one person in a crowd of thousands looks straight at the camera.
Instead of a sentence you could just build a shelf. For the 40th time I died
trying to break in to the collectors' convention. My city is custom, my
language is custom, I built the maps from an ancient graveyard. I don't
know my own number. I enjoy the music of ice cubes. When my prince
came on a plane I heard his soft thunder. I searched for Los Angeles, and a
few other places, but ended up here, in the one city they decided to raze.
I relax by playing a stressful game. I want to see your side of the version.
I praise the back of a painting. I see consciousness as a pond-shaped,
deepening dip that I can feel myself occupy as I fall asleep. I had plans
for words that never came to anything. I even had words for the storm's
architecture. I copied your notes. They just use rain to erase the tall build-
ings. We're not so different, the system and me. With all the huge ads and
bouts of consumption I felt like I was in Britain or something. The boys
stand without moving in tiny white cubicles, still believing they're being
considered. The youth all have that Aryan look. If the talk is too boring I
like to imagine Levin's pioneering use of the acronym. When cleaning a
staircase I leave one step unswept, just to compare with. Everything I've
ever loved fits in your silhouette. I get collector's envy. A glass breaks
when I remember your name, but not because I remember your name.
The shelves are all sanded, but it's a question in practice of deciding what

not to put on them. Not this, it's too male. The sign says I'm out to meet an unplanned event. Please do not contact me with offers or services. For now my tribute remains this side of the virtual. I ran down the darkened passageway to receive my scar. I will never say this out loud.

from *The Poetry Review*

where the heart is streaming

◊　◊　◊

there are places in which the mind thrives like plankton, where jobs
are easy to come by & every apartment overlooks the park, where
the funeral has barely started & the heart is a mist that rises & clears
like a browser & streaming faster – a gapless surface of fake solids

& there are places in which love reproduces itself like a lizard's tail, heeds
to no alarm or database. places where the sun rises like a fat cunt
glowing in the sky. places where the rats don't race but rat out
their days in a waterlogged stupor. places you can dive into from a height

there are places where a heart is megashared & its kitchens always full
of foods. where babies name themselves. a place you cannot unknow
& in some place from the past there is a bucket doubling as a womb, full
of infant newts & frogspawn. in some place you cannot know is you

full to the brim with ungendered yearning. & there are places that smell
of honey & decay, places where mistakes can be undone by pressing
a sequence of two or three keys. places where the language flows uncoded,
where everybody understands each other. there are places where people

burn money to keep warm, places where every shop window is broken & blood
makes patterns on the walls. there are places where every building looks
the same & nothing can be bought or sold. there are places through which
a tall fence runs with holes too small to kiss your opposite number

& there are places in which each citizen is tattooed, head to toe, with the face
& body of another citizen & everybody takes to the lakes naked, places
where public transport is free & police tip their hats to beggars on the streets
& nobody dies. there are places where the dead rise from their graves

& avenge the living, places where the dead turn into doves just to peck
themselves dead again. there are places in which bleeding takes the place

of talking, places with water in place of mirrors, with eyes instead of cameras,
patches of pure darkness on a google map, places you can't arrive or leave

& there are places in which the lives of happy & boring people unfold
day after day, where nobody writes anything down & nobody suffers
from the damp & cold. there are places you have been & will
never go again, where the yearning to visit stands in for the visiting

as though you could trick yourself out of death or labour for a second
go at being free. there are places where the moon is god-blocked into
a pinprick, & places where it largens & honeys, places night never falls
& the citizens sleep with snakes across their eyes to block the light

& the heart itself a snake knotted into a place we can never see or fathom
a stupid fist raised in protest, shrinking by the minute, longing to be dropped
in steaming water, to expand to the size of a glass like a hybrid tea rose sewn
together in a factory in bangladesh & sold for eight hundred times its worth

& the workers streaming utopia their bodies dropping from the walls all night

from the *Morning Star*

Poem In Which I Watch Jane Brakhage Give Birth

◇ ◇ ◇

Baby's debut in bath water
head crowning and Jane has her mouth open
it's as if the first baby of Earth is being born now
it hurts my vagina but it is not my vagina
I clench it shut.

Stan is behind the camera and I wonder
if Daddy is missing the whole thing
or if he realises he is Daddy yet.
The year is 1958.

I want to name her Agnes but she is not mine
Baby's head is crowning
it hurts and I clench again.
My mind goes to the black cherries and rice pudding
I had for dessert at lunch.

Baby's debut and we see the window,
so off to the garden now, off now
Baby is four years old
how fast it all went by
when the film is not even over yet.

from *Poems in Which*

Elegy for Olive Oyl

◇ ◇ ◇

I'll go back to painters and whistles, shipwreck gardens,
Turk's Heads, leaden hearts and let the winds their revels keep.

I'll go back to the water for something to put the ghost back
in me, as no one says. Your body gestured commensurate with

mastheads asway blindingly against the sun, sowing sunspots on
the horizon: I bears this image in mind. You, and you

knowing all your dazzled life that nothing always haunts at its edges
something, being much larger and altogether more convincing.

I bears in mind your grey camisole the morning we almost married.
I singing into your sleep like a pebble lobbed at your bedroom window.

I sang up a work song, you threw me a dresser.
                              I sang up a work song I'm working to finish.

My first language was Sailortown pidgin, my palette's on fire with salt.
My sweetest voice still is vinegared plums, a thousand tobacco plugs

stiffen my tongue.
                    The sad-sackery of all this doesn't escape me.
My posy wilts at the cold milk bottle: spilling is in its essence so it spills.

The knot weakens the rope. If we won't marry, retell me the dream of twins –
each of them was me you said their breaths rattled your clapboard walls

you said their forearms were the size of melons you said.
I haven't thrown a punch in years now the old buffoon is underground.

I can't put my arms to work, my chest is tight as frozen oak.

There's nothing here for me to haunt – I bears this in mind.

I anticipate better weather but there's no sea change –
the sea being always water. Once, I folded

a ship's overbite over itself; propellers twirled like pinwheels.
Laugh like that again! & let the winds their revels keep.

I want to be light as every floating thing.
I'm ready to shove off. I'm ready, I promise.

I've been trying to eat more spinach.

from *Poetry London*

O blinde Augen

◇ ◇ ◇

My voice
my voice alone
will touch you
from crown to heel
a glass of Siberian champagne
downed in one –
As the storm takes the coast
to its breast
my voice will bring you back
our vanished day –
As the sea surges over the freeway
my voice will flow to you
on bended knee –

My voice will tend you
like a child raised by wolves

All this is true
and now
I will tell you one of my lies
    beloved
as I used to
and you always understood

from *The Rialto*

from *The Kathy Doll*

◇ ◇ ◇

Kathy didn't want to be a tract, wasn't able to hope for broken glass she was in prison, comely little girl completely mad. Kathy has been lots of places, she plet her tongue before locating her desires and when she disappeared she pleted the ocean.

Kathy was neither shame nor guilt nor plom she would plop her worn out cunt. She would mop up her father and mother and join us for a tea party. Kathy would mope for hours each day in front of the telly. She would peel the skin from the corner of her lips blow it towards me and I would come with her dusty skin falling all around me.

Kathy had a plant and she called it Kathy. An ant climbed all over the leaves a little map that Kathy would read when she needed more words in her liant Kathy was a liar and she always told the truth. Kathy had pliant legs and strong hands and an overly sensitive clitoris.

Kathy said amen once and then laughed just because she was able to blame someone at last, God is so blamable, so invisible, so sive. I've sap from Kathy's skin in a tiny test tube and I sip it when I need a bit of vis scattered about the cold room.

Kathy is a sieve I use sometimes when I need a sign, every one of Kathy's books is signed with need with gen with sing at pat at patterns. Kathy used a net to make stories and Kathy had natty tits hidden in a tent top until needed.

Kathy had a dol called Kathy, a cile dol with oil in her hair, a tame dol with Kathy arms the dol was maim and had me taken out of her palms and Kathy drank tea when she was in London, sitting on her bed, I sud next to her and I would sub tea with her and I am not ded bud she is and when I sued Kathy for stealing my words she told me she was due and that it was time to deliver her.

'How much pain are you willing to experience?' Kathy asked me.

She explained that she wanted to hold out her arms inside me and push and push and push until I start shaking.

'Hurt me baby, show me what love is,' I told my Kathy child.

Kathy is a building in which the windows and doors no longer exist.

from *Blackbox Manifold*

The Underground

◊ ◊ ◊

My grandfather clipped
hedges in Northern
Ireland.
My great grandfather
was a gardener
for rich Anglo Irish.
My mother is a cleaner.
My stepfather
fixes air conditioners.
My biological father
was a gardener
in Belfast.
They cut off
one of his toes.
I have a bad toe.
I have a bad knee.
I am tracing
my ancestry.
I like the ground.
I come from the ground.
The earth peoples
like an apple tree apples
says Alan Watts.
It's 5.23.
Sirens are going off.
I ride the underground.
I come from working
class roots.
Who doesn't?
I do not know
how to hammer.
When I worked

construction
I could not find
the stud.
I am not a man.
I am not a woman.
I am riding the
underground.
Where does it go?
Nobody knows.

from *Lighthouse*

Letter from Sido

◊　◊　◊

So, my very dear mother, speak on the verge of death, speak in the name of your
inflexible standards, in the name of the unique virtue that you called 'true elegance
of behaviour'
– Colette

I'm writing this by the light of a barn
in flames, Madame Moreau's. One wonders,
with the old man gone and her gout getting worse.
I see the poor rats running all over the garden.
How beautiful it all is!
I saw old Loeuvrier go by last week
in his coffin. I do like watching funerals,
one can always learn from them.
But don't ever let me see you in mourning for me,
you know how I loathe black – what's wrong with pink?
I've been making a big bed-jacket from an old pink quilt.
I want to be buried in it. Thank you for your invitation.
No, Josephine is *not* sleeping in the house.
I sleep here alone, so please, no more fuss.
No more stories of wicked tramps kicking down the door.
Give me a dog if you like.
Ever since your father died I cannot bear
another human being in the house at night.
Dear child, you write that you're not well,
is it the city, the air too thick and sour?
Do you remember that time I went to the Curé
in a fury about something only to dance home
with that beautiful Pelargonium cutting he gave me?
This time he gave me a cactus – it's here on the sill.
Beyond it I can see the blaze dying down.
I keep waking up. The other morning at three
I watched a very handsome garden spider slowly

descend and drink from my blue bowl then draw
herself, heavy with chocolate, back up to the ceiling.
Et voilà! a new companion.
I've been going through the books on your father's shelves.
It's such a bore – all the love in them.
In real life, my poor Minet-Chéri, folk have better things to do.
I hear from your brothers – so you write about your life?
You see? I warned you about going to confession,
I always said it led a child to play around too much
with words, make things up, navel-gaze.
Better to hold your tongue – punish yourself yourself.
This cactus is very rare. It's pink.
And the Curé says it's about to come out.
As I write, a stray is winding her way round my ankles.
She looks quite blue in the glow. I'll cook her an egg.
I did the same for poor Yvette's girl the other day.
I don't do it because I'm good, heaven knows.
I do what'll set my mind at rest – you know me.
The other day I found a caterpillar hibernating,
a bird had pecked out her stomach.
I have her healing now in a little matchbox of sand
on my bedside table – what a beauty she'll be
and all the more so for having suffered!
There's just black sky now where the barn was.
You know the worst thing about being old?
– the sight of my hand on the sheet.
I still play chess with my little wool-seller.
Your father would have been delighted,
the dead are a peaceful company, my child.
The Curé tells me this cactus only flowers once
every four years. And I am dying.
You will forgive me, won't you, Minet-Chéri,
you will understand that I can't come to you.
You who took three days and three nights to leave my body.
Children like you are the most beloved because
they've lain so high, so close to the mother's heart.
I can hear my pen scratching in the dark.
I have grown very thin.
When I'm at the water pump in the morning
I feel my dress touch the backs of my legs,
the sun is just warm and I feel ten years old.
How can I leave now?
How could I leave that thing to flower alone?

Someone needs to see it into the world.
I want it to be me peering into its closed pink heart.
I want to watch it push its slow suddenness
out and quiver there in the warm air.

from *The Poetry Review*

The Leopard-God

◇ ◇ ◇

Came the Leopard-God
in a cape of beech leaves:
from one shore to the other
he passed at night,
with Nicholas on his back
clutching the fur and crying,
come again, come back,
pulling at the linty ears
of the Leopard-God – who
never gets angry, or at least
not with Nicholas, his own
blond boy, his refugee – his
little, his ever-so-patient love.

from *clinic*

Flame Brocade Moth

from 'Extinct Species of the British Isles'

◊　◊　◊

1919

I was unsure what to say to a person
who was in the process of dying
my chest hurt and my eyes hurt
it was a very bright day
my friend was on the lip of the
world
her hair looked awful

my friend stayed in her chair
but she was gathering up the
leaves outside
she was gathering up the branches
the snow before anyone else has looked
at it
the thin peels of rain
the gutted fish
the orange ball which fell behind the
shed in 2007
the puddle full of motorcycle oil

my womb was throbbing
to remake her
but she was doing it herself

there was a fire and it cleared
the forest floor of bracken
clean dirty burning
this unwieldy flood

from *B O DY*

JACK UNDERWOOD

Accidental Narratives

◊   ◊   ◊

A crab on the phone box floor; the armless mannequin
on the chapel roof at dawn; the plastic toad in the office
biscuit tin; three cuts on your shin this morning to make
the letter A; the wedding cake abandoned in the car park
of the motorway services; the caraway seed in the turn-up
of your jeans, the waxwork head of Chaplin in the bowling
bag in the overhead locker of the night train to Munich;
a slug exposed by the spotlight of a hushed concert hall;
or the roaring magnificent intersection of these objects,
which probably never existed, but we can each picture,
drawn from our unique worlds at large, knocking like fish,
trying to agree; meanwhile, either somebody else somewhere
is reading this now, or no one else in the entire world is.

from the *New Statesman*

MARK WALDRON

I am lordly, puce and done,

◊ ◊ ◊

but enough about me, Manning says
as he adjust his tights under what we take for a moon.

There's a cascading swagger,
everything is joy in a thin strip:

*Forgive me, the trees themselves
are morose rather than lightweight, the sky is certainly lit.
The ground bows down like a dumpty stone
quite free under its own buff
beneath the undressed yellowy pomp of its own boff,*
and Manning laughs a luvvy laugh beneath a stony arch.

Marcie is all light of course and buzzing honey,
though quite as quiet as my open hand
and my old forgotten blood
who sings to himself
as he trundles about
picking up oxygen
spending it wisely
driving the pump that pumps him round
picking it up again
spending it wisely
singing the red corpuscle song.

The made-bees are quite as quiet as the blown-mice
(all my house is glass),
and Marcie is just about as clean as any window
ever was.
No so sorry dirt at all for me to make my home in.

from *Prac Crit*

121

Losing Lion

◊   ◊   ◊

was the worst thing that ever happened to me.
What soft dreams I had, waking up to his golden mane
his smell of far away sun.

We should have looked for him longer, I always felt
he was just in the next aisle as we looked
not quite quickly enough to catch up,

maybe someone hid him under a shelf.
Afterwards Agnes died.
You left to be pregnant hours away on the train

and when I visit at weekends you hold my hair as if I am Lion.

from *Poetry Wales*

Mort Dieu

◇ ◇ ◇

Our son
dear God
is dead
and gone.
His tomb
was red
with blood
and warm
as tears.
He was
born still.
Was this
dear God
your will?

from *Ink, Sweat & Tears*

Losing It

◊ ◊ ◊

It comes to something
when you are so afraid
of mislaying your possessions
you find yourself

roping your bed to the floor
with a running bowline
and every chair in the room

is knotted to a wall
with a sheet bend and you can no longer
open your wardrobe door
because you've spliced it to the curtains

with a round turn
and two half hitches.
There must be a storm coming in
dad, now that everything in your flat
is lashed down. You are
as you tell me, at sea
and I agree. After years

twisting nets in fishing ports
you have plaited all the lanyards
of your life together

here in the secure unit
at Wootton Lawn. At last you're
tied down, have nothing left to lose
except your mind
to which I am so attached

I keep coming back
to hear you list
all the things you've lost
and whatever else you've forgotten

to recall including the common ground
we've found in making lists
as we slip between unfinished
sentences, pass each other
spare syllables, are lost
for words.

from *Poetry London*

CONTRIBUTORS' NOTES AND COMMENTS

ARIA ABER is a recent English Literature graduate from Goldsmiths College, University of London. Her work has appeared in journals like *Lighthouse, PANK, Wasafiri, decomP* and others. She was awarded the Wasafiri New Writing Prize in Poetry and is the recipient of a *MIEL* fellowship. She serves as a poetry reader for *The Adroit Journal*. She writes, 'The perspective this poem is written from automatically bleeds into political realms. I will never forget my father's voice when he said he wished Afghanistan had at least been colonised in the course of its destruction. Perspective is everything, and often ushers irony into tragedy. "First Generation Immigrant Child" serves as an attempt to investigate the disparate spaces of an immigrant experience – the seemingly contradictory aspects are kept in cohesion by the use of anaphora, reverberating the existential question of what it means to be a woman, an outsider, a foreigner in both the new and the old culture – this poem is a simple, blunt mirror of an identity crisis between Occident and Orient, between rejection of ethnicity and simultaneous self-exoticisation; an alternative title could have been "Self-Portrait as Orientalism".'

ASTRID ALBEN's most recent collection *Ai! Ai! Pianissimo* was published by Arc Publications in 2011. Alben has been described as 'a new and original voice in English poetry, serious and uncompromising' (*TLS*). Her poems, translations and reviews are widely published, and her poetry is translated into several languages, including Romanian, Slovenian and Chinese. Alben is the editor of three art-science anthologies: *Findings on Ice* (2007), *Findings on Elasticity* (2010) and *Findings on Light* (2015), published by Lars Müller Publications. Her next collection, *Plainspeak*, an alter-ego-thinker-out-louder book, will be ready this year. Alben is an RSA and Wellcome Trust Fellow. She comments, 'Since "One of the Guys" appeared in the *TLS* people have asked, "So, go on, Astrid, who's the poet?" My answer has been consistent: "The poet? That would be me.'"

RACHAEL ALLEN studied English Literature at Goldsmiths College, University of London. Her poetry has appeared or is forthcoming in *Poetry London* and *The Poetry Review*, and a pamphlet of her poems is published by Faber & Faber. Her reviews and essays have appeared in *Ambit* magazine, *Dazed & Confused* and *Music & Literature*. She is the poetry editor for *Granta*, co-editor of poetry anthology series *clinic* and of online journal *tender*. Rachael notes, 'I read Selima Hill's "Prawns de Jo" when I was fifteen and it was one of the first poems that illuminated me as to what poetry is capable of – a rewriting of an emotion I thought I knew. From the first stanza I was hooked on the poem:

'Because she was wrong,
because it was all her fault right from the beginning,
because she was ashamed of even thinking about it,
and should never have been his daughter in the first place;
because she was ugly
and he was magnificent
and she was the scum of the earth

'When you're a fifteen-year-old girl, when you're a woman, feelings of shame are mandatory; it was the feeling I felt and probably still feel the most. What Selima Hill's poem goes on to talk about – singeing babies, pet pubic hair, things we are "secretly proud of because we are horrified by" – introduced me to a way of talking about our shame and what triggers it. A feeling not exclusive to women, but one we are encouraged to feel. There's much we aren't supposed to think about but we all inevitably and definitely do, but would never admit to, and may even chastise if we heard them spoken from others. I wrote my poem a short while after I had been left for someone else, and the shame within me was hot and palpable and glowing and I imagined everyone could see it. Writing the poem back to Hill I felt as though I was one in a billion women feeling shame and working with her strange pattern exorcised the feelings. That the person who'd left me was called Joe was just one of those happy coincidences.'

JANETTE AYACHI (*b.* 1982) is a Scottish-Algerian London-born Edinburgh-based poet with an MSc in Creative Writing from Edinburgh University, and a combined BA Honours in English Literature and Film/Media Studies from Stirling University. She has been widely published in over fifty literary journals and anthologies including *New Writing Scotland*, *Gutter*, *The Istanbul Review*, *Magma*, *Be the First to Like This: New*

Scottish Poetry and *Out There: Anthology of LGBT Writers*. She was short-listed for Write Queer London and a Lancelot Andrewes Award, and is the winner of the Barbara Burford prize from The Young Enigma Awards 2014. She edits the online arts journal *The Undertow Review* and performs her poetry across the UK. She is the author of poetry pamphlets *Pauses at Zebra Crossings* and *A Choir of Ghosts*, and currently working on her first full poetry book *Hand Over Mouth Music*. She comments as follows, 'This poem wears no masks; it is an open-plan love poem, an ode to the synergy and passion between poets, a letter of seduction, a glass raised to the "chlorinated friendship" between women, a document of unrequited desire and an unravelling of the beast within us all, as it rises to the surface, itching to howl.'

TARA BERGIN is from Dublin, but is currently living in Northern England. Her first collection of poems, *This is Yarrow*, was published by Carcanet in 2013, and was awarded the Seamus Heaney Centre for Poetry Prize, and the Shine/Strong Award for best first collection by an Irish author. In 2014 she was named a PBS Next Generation poet. She writes, 'A trip to the hairdresser gave me this poem. It represents a moment in time in which something ordinary and irrelevant suddenly seemed to capture something quite the opposite. In terms of drafting, I needed to do relatively little. Essentially, it was a case of knowing for some time what I wanted to say, but not knowing how, until the normal ritual of going to get my hair cut unexpectedly offered me a way. But I suspect that the experience of going to the hairdresser is one that many writers find both alarming and enthralling: it is an experience of surrender, physical and intellectual, and because of this, offers an opportunity to practice the simple but essential tasks of observation and description.'

CRISPIN BEST lives in London and at www.crispinbest.com. He notes, 'The poem is built around an image, borrowed from Donald Revell's "A Branch of the Discipline", of nesting herons killed by thunderstorms. I wrote the poem shortly after learning what an orrery is while looking at one in the British Museum. The orrery I saw was tremendously sad and built in the late 1700s. An orrery is a clockwork model of the solar system. At the time of writing, there are over 400,000 lbs' worth of human detritus on the moon, including a feather, a cast gold olive branch, a tiny aluminium memorial bearing the names of 14 dead astronauts, and almost a hundred bags of urine, faeces and vomit. There is something both ter-rifying and peaceful about everything.'

A. K. BLAKEMORE was named a Foyle Young Poet of the Year in 2008 and 2009, and had her work published in a variety of zines and journals.

Her first full-length collection, *Humbert Summer*, was released by Eyewear in 2015. She currently lives and works in South-east London. She comments, 'It's probably not the right thing to say but this poem might be one of the things I wrote in the past year that, in retrospect, I enjoy least. This might partly be because the circumstances in which I wrote it – predictably, the disintegration of a long-term relationship – make it difficult for me to see it through the eyes of a less involved party. Primarily, I think I might not like it because it is a poem about being cowardly, and the desire to put distance between ourselves and the people we know we have hurt so we don't have to confront anything or one. The imagery is drawn from trips to the countryside real and semi-imaginary. We're still friends.'

SARAH BOULTON is an artist and poet-writer living in London and recently graduated from the Slade School of Art. She is 1/4 of *LOW IMPACT*, an art publication and is 1/2 of Living and Love, a music and lyric writing collaboration with James Lowne. Her poetry has been published in *tender* (2015) and recent shows include *Mark II* held in a Nissan Micra car, and birdsneedgravitytoswallow.org (2014). Her tumblr is saraboulton.tumblr.com. She writes, '"Powder" became a poem/fairytale in that the work dissolved into its form as time went on and as I wrote it down. Previously it really was just on my nails and showed-told some people about it. I also had this small ambiguous label-less bottle with a chalky thick white substance in it that I felt not very interested in. I preferred the relationship between the stone/her work that dissolved and the words, which kind of started to feel like the powdered-down version of some very clearly laid out scenario.'

KIT BUCHAN is a poet and journalist whose poems have appeared in *clinic*, *The White Review* and *Five Dials*. Besides poetry, he writes song lyrics, and has recently completed a musical, *Newfrock*, with the composer Jim Barne. He works for *The Observer*'s science pages, and is currently preparing a series of poetry broadcasts for Resonance FM. Kit comments as follows, 'As you can see, this poem is about how men behave in pubs. The pub is a kind of panic-room for some of the men I've known, like a cosy Anderson-shelter full of wooden fittings and wobbly beer. They go there – let's face it – to cower from women, women being the main obstacle to the perseverance of their dubious self-images. Like these men, I used to think of pubs as solid, unpretentious places, but increasingly they strike me as quite camp.

'They've got funny names, like theatres do, and all over the country little plays are happening inside them; improvised mood-pieces performed by groups of two or more men, with each man emphatically reprising his role as a stalwart, no-bullshit booze-mensch – his audience his fellow actors. There's lighting and a soundtrack and props and so on.

'I have taken (still take!) part in this dispiriting little drama more frequently than I'd care to calculate, and it's an exhausting procedure. It's like a staring-contest: who's going to blink first, break character and go home, ruining it.

'More so than any of my other poems, this one incites people – always men – to come up after a reading and speak to me. They say "Ah man, I know that guy. His name's Chris and I'm going to the fucking pub with him tomorrow; I don't know why I do it!" I am always pleased to hear this, because it's flattering and I know the feeling, but if I'm in a particularly generous mood, I wonder whether Chris might not be preparing for the encounter with equal dread.'

SAM BUCHAN-WATTS is a founding editor of the anthology series *clinic*. His poetry appears in *Poetry London*, *Ambit*, *Lighthouse*, and *The Best British Poetry 2013*, and his articles in *i-D*, *Dazed & Confused*, *PN Review*, and elsewhere.

He writes, 'Having grown up not far from a plate-glass university, its pigeon-grey Modernist buildings and hilly environs proved to be a continual source of bafflement to my early-teens self (it gave me a sense of the bureaucratic before I could properly pin meaning to that word). And a useful one at that: I went mostly during summer holidays, and it provided secluded spots to pitch £9.99 Argos tents on, tall grass to smoke weed in, and the right concrete banks and steps for skateboarding. (Some kid let off a fire extinguisher in our tent the night we camped, so we went to A&E.) I did once skate past a medieval reenactment on my way home, which struck me, even at the age of fifteen, as a beautiful and absurd thing to have been allowed to see; made better by the fact that it was in passing, and the wind was loud, and I could have missed it. The title was a phrase spoken by a friend who clicked his fingers and said "the days go just like that" (these days being rare, as he was referring to a working life in a room with no windows), or it may have been "the days *just go* like that", I can't remember. There's a sequel to this poem which uses this other title, "The days just go like that", but the same template, except it looks backward, re-submerging into the woods, in search of the metropolis on the other side. I would say it's in reverse but the days are irreversible.'

MILES BURROWS was born in Leicester and studied Russian in the National Service – they had to learn Russian folk songs so they could sing them in case they were caught by the Russians and suspected of being spies. He studied Classics and then Medicine, and wrote reviews for the *New Statesman*. His collection *A Vulture's Egg* was published by Cape in

1966. He has been anthologised in *British Poetry since 1945*. Recent poems have appeared in *Poetry Review, TLS* and *PN Review*. He writes, '"Letter to an an Elderly Poet" is a response to Virginia Woolf's "Letter to a Young Poet". It means don't be writing poems at this age. It's like putting on a rugby shirt and racing round empty stadiums at night. Whatever you do at this age is not going to look good. Even bowls has something comical about it, at any age. You should be washing up in a corner or telling stories about your grandparents to your grandchildren. Chekhov laughed at a man for playing the cello at the age of forty. (Though Anthony Powell has a more sympathetic portrait of his aged General Conyers on the cello.) The poem is in the didactic mode, like Elizabeth David, Mrs Beeton, Ovid's *Art of Love*, Peter Porter's "How to Get a Girlfriend".

'The rhythm has several Latinate hexameters. Also caesuras and quite a lot of end stops. And some rhythms remisicent of Theodore Roethke's ("carry me further back . . ."). "Let your trembling hand . . .": When life drawing with an especially beautiful model the hand may start to shake. If you can't control this try incorporating the tremor into the picture as an expression of mood. "The Chinese sage": A scroll in our dining room, showing a tubby half-bald pot-bellied little old man smiling happily as he sweeps with a broom. (He is the monk-poet Szih-De, lived during the T'ang Dynasty (618–907).) The picture is covered with the red seals of emperors who have been captivated by it. It is done with a brush loaded with dilute ink and a few broad strokes liberally applied. The smile is done with a single line. The face seems to be shining. You might imagine he is punting a gondola. "That terrible cry": We have a back garden not far from a river, and the cry was heard in the middle of writing the poem. It may well have been ducks. Chekhov loves to put incidental inanimate noises into his plays: the noise in the stove the night father died, the nightwatchman's stick, the noise like a violin string breaking.'

NIALL CAMPBELL is a Scottish poet originally from the island of South Uist, one of the Outer Hebrides of Scotland. He has been a recipient of an Eric Gregory Award (2011) and a Robert Louis Stevenson Fellowship (2011). *Moontide*, his first collection, is published by Bloodaxe, and was named inaugural winner of the £20,000 Edwin Morgan Poetry Award (2014), and received the Saltire First Book of the Year Award (2014). *Moontide* was also shortlisted for both the Forward and the Fenton Aldeburgh Prizes for Best First Collection, and given a Poetry Book Society Recommendation. He comments, 'This poem was written a few months after my son was born. Late nights, let's say, were not uncommon during this period. On one of these night/mornings I was walking through the rooms remembering how in an epigraph to a John Glenday poem it was stated that the sound a heart makes while beating is 'lub–dub'. And it is, isn't it? But I was always a bit more interested in what things are heard to be, rather than necessarily *are*. And I heard it beating as the "oh heart, poor heart" refrain that beats through the poem. A bit overawed by love, and a bit overawed by the recent change in my life – I tried to use this steady beat as the framework for a poem that is about being unbalanced – at a turning point, and being well into turning.'

VAHNI CAPILDEO (*b*. Trinidad) writes across genres. Recent work can be found in *Utter* (Peepal Tree, 2013), *New Poetries VI* (Carcanet, 2015), *Simple Complex Shapes* (Shearsman, 2015) and *Measures of Expatriation* (Carcanet, forthcoming 2016). As Judith E. Wilson Fellow 2014 at the University of Cambridge, she intensified her collaborative and multidimensional work, with a particular interest in long-duration and/or immersive events including text. She notes, 'The mosses in this piece of writing derive from moss in Trinidad, Iceland, and Oxford. The layering of place via embodied memory informs both content and shape. This may produce a wayward or confusing effect, though the form is bounded and the language controlled, if the reader(s) are accustomed to anecdotal or memoiristic poems. The feeling of recollection-in-apprehension, place-through-place, times-in-time, is equal and immediate in life, so misleadingly slow and complex to account for in writing, perhaps quicker to compress into poetry that tries not to mimic, but rather to replicate, such texturing in some possible reading experiences. The Port of Spain family home had been invaded in various ways. My father's sister's husband was a botanist in Berkeley, California, and whether with cavalier experimentalism or with a researcher's care, gave us seeds and spores to sow. It was in looking for alien ferns that I began to focus on the habitats of moss (also the habitats of assorted reptiles), beneath the ixoras and near the hole leading to the deep drain down which a market crab intended for boiling once escaped, claws held aloft like a supporter of Spartacus. The green of a shallow in the lawn where fatigued builders had dumped a load of concrete owed more to moss than grass; I had no real pets and patted it quite often, playing alone, loving its dense fuzz. Later, I marvelled at the variety of mosses on the lava fields of Iceland, and felt awe and pity at a breakable, beautiful friend who slipped with bad results on ill-tended stone in Oxford. The piece belongs to an evolving set of writings, in conversation with the writer and performer Maya Chowdhry, with whom I have spent happy times talking ecology, having ice cream for breakfast in Manchester, admiring a stone wall in Edinburgh, and tearing up shared and unshared assumptions on how to write, well, about things.'

KAYO CHINGONYI is a fellow of the Complete Works programme for diversity and quality in British poetry and the author of two pamphlets, *Some Bright Elegance* (Salt, 2012) and *The Colour of James Brown's Scream* (Akashic, 2016). He represented Zambia at Poetry Parnassus, won the 2012 Geoffrey Dearmer Prize, and was awarded a residency at Cove Park to work on his debut full-length collection, *Kumukanda*. He will be Associate Poet at the ICA from Autumn 2015 to Spring 2016. He notes the following, '"Legerdemain" is one of a number of poems I've written in other voices and might be something of a companion to a poem in my first pamphlet called "How To Build Cathedrals". I was interested, in both poems, with inhabiting a position that is very different from my own (in both cases I couldn't quite commit fully in terms of tone but I suppose irony is a part of these poems too).

'"Legerdemain" was written for an event called "Discomfort Zone". Each of the poets performing was asked to write something based on a subject suggested for them by someone else. The whole idea was that this subject should be something outside of the commissioned poet's comfort zone and sure enough I was given "cigars". This, I have to admit, wasn't as fiendish a brief as some but I didn't have any real point of ingress to the subject, being somewhat averse to cigar smoke and smoking generally. For a while I kept going back to Freud and Groucho Marx but these seemed too easy, somehow, since the associations are well established in popular culture.

'I knew I wanted to take a different tack but nothing was forthcoming until I came across a passage in Adam Hochschild's book, *King Leopold's Ghost*, that referred to an open letter written by George Washington Williams to King Leopold II. I had to seize on the opportunity since it felt like a gift. In the letter Washington Williams describes how Leopold's officials used cigars and magnifying glasses, among other tricks, to secure rights to land in the Congo. The title had been in my mind for years as I love the way the word sounds and, after the excitement of finding a way in, the poem came very quickly.'

SOPHIE COLLINS is co-founder and editor of *tender*, an online quarterly promoting work by female-identified writers and artists. Her poems have appeared in *Poetry*, *Poetry London*, *The White Review*, *Ploughshares*, *Poetic Series* (Sternberg Press), and elsewhere. She received an Eric Gregory Award in 2014, and is now editing *Currently & Emotion*, an anthology of translations to be published by Test Centre in early 2016. Her first collection will be published by Penguin in 2017. She writes, 'The poem concerns one of my favourite *Simpsons* characters Selma Bouvier, of misandrist, chain-smoking twins Patty and Selma. Selma is the eldest of the twins by two minutes. Her name means "divine helmet" at its Germanic origins. Together the sisters are perceived as sucking the life out of everything.'

CLAIRE CROWTHER has published three collections of poetry, including *On Narrowness* (Shearsman, 2015), and four pamphlets including *Silents* (Hercules Editions, 2015). She is poet in residence at the Royal Mint Museum 2014–2015. She notes, 'The last stanza of "Week of Flies, 1968" is autobiography. I was a student at Manchester University, running round the capitals of Europe demonstrating, when I wasn't sitting in, as we used to say, in whichever offices of Manchester University we sat in. That particular year, I wrote poems about manual workers and worked as a factory cleaner for several months. The rest of this poem tries to capture the mixture of violence and nurture that is revolution. (And is self-definition for each generation.) I wrote it out of a moment of attention to the state of the world so many years after the visionary conversations I had had then and after listening to similar conversations being held now. I turned twenty-one in 1968. The world was forty-five years older when I finished writing this poem.'

PAULA CUNNINGHAM lives in Belfast. Smith/Doorstop have published a chapbook, *A Dog Called Chance* (1999) and *Heimlich's Manoeuvre* (2013), which was shortlisted for the Fenton-Aldeburgh, Seamus Heaney Centre, and Strong Shine First Collection Prizes. Her short story 'The Matchboy' won second prize in the 2014 Costa Short Story Award. She has also written drama. Her work appears in print and online journals in the UK and Ireland, Europe, Canada and the US, and has been widely anthologised. She has received awards from the Arts Council of Northern Ireland and features in their online Troubles Archive. She writes, 'I work as a dentist in Belfast, treating adults and children with disabilities and complex medical needs. I take a comprehensive medical history for all of my patients. From time to time this elicits stories which are rich, urgent, and highly charged. The speaker's words tumble over each other and the air in my surgery fizzes, leaving me humbled and awed. The poem is an attempt to capture something of this, and is an anonymised and re-imagined amalgam (!) of stories I have encountered.

'Snow is a potent symbol in Irish literature. I particularly thought of Gabriel Conroy, standing by the window, towards the end of James Joyce's "The Dead". This led me on, and I had fun trying to shoehorn allusions to poems and poets into the final three stanzas, making it a history of snow in that sense also.

'It was important to me to capture the working-class Belfast vernacular. I don't speak this myself, and it presented a challenge – to be faithful without being patronising. It caused me some anxiety, so I'm especially delighted to have the poem re-presented here. I'm also grateful to PNR and the Hippocrates Poetry Prize 2014, who awarded it third place in the NHS category.'

JESSE DARLING is an artist and occasional poet living and working in London. Jesse writes, 'This text has been edited and excerpted from a group Google document in which the members of the collective formerly known as Grand George used to catalogue their dreams in between meetings. Grand George was a collective formed around the collaborative attempt to create a new religion, using bibliomancy and geometry as well as dream mapping to form a framework for rituals and belief systems. The collective exists today under a new name, though Jesse Darling is no longer a member. All text reproduced here was produced by the subconscious of Jesse Darling (possibly in collaboration with the subconscious of other members of the original group, or maybe not). Any resemblance to persons living or dead or events in the past or future is unintentional, though perhaps inevitable.'

PATRICIA DEBNEY's recent publications include *Gestation* (Shearsman Chapbooks, 2014) and a collection of prose poems, *Littoral* (Shearsman Books, 2013). Her first collection, *How to Be a Dragonfly* (Smith/Doorstop Books), won the 2004 Poetry Business Book & Pamphlet Competition; her next collection *Baby* is published by Liquorice Fish Books in 2016. A former Canterbury Laureate, she is Reader in Creative Writing at the University of Kent. She notes, 'This poem is the first in a small series of "Dreams" included in my next collection. As a whole, the book explores parental relationships, aging, dementia, and fragmentation. Many of the poems in this book have emerged in "layered" stanzas of various patterns. Looking back now, I wonder if I located these patterns as ways of privileging sonic/rhythmic and vertical connections over the seductive – yet for me, less authentic in this case – tug toward "resolution". I think I wanted the poems – like relationships – to remain porous. This move into lineated poetry is a shift for me, and about a third of the pieces in *Baby* are in my more usual mode, prose poetry – though too, the prose poems are voice rather than narrative oriented. *Baby* was drafted very quickly over several weeks, a disorienting but revealing process: through this I came to know that these memories, these voices and dreams, were all I had to try to understand – accept? – where I and we are now.'

IAN DUHIG has written six books of poetry, most recently *Pandorama* (Picador, 2010) while his seventh, *The Blind Roadmaker* – which will include this poem – is forthcoming, also from Picador. He has won the Forward Best Poem Prize, the National Poetry Competition twice and three times been shortlisted for the T.S. Eliot Prize. Ian writes, 'This started from Sam Gwynn's Ashbery parody "The Rum District". Although I like Ashbery, I've always found parodies inspiring and wrote about Ern Malley in my first book. My poem, so, is a reflection of a reflection, recursive like the mirrors de Selby sets up opposite each other to investigate time-travel in Flann O'Brien's *The Third Policeman*, a rum book itself. "Rum", "Room" and "Rûm" can be puns in Northern English, the last (derived from "Rome") being the early Muslim name for Byzantium, that Roman and Greek city, its territories (such as Romania) and by extension Christianity in general – a flexible term like the Arabic *beit*, the metrical unit corresponding to a poem's line, but which can be rendered as "a couplet", another suggestive doubling to me. *Beit* nowadays means "house", but originally "tent" (the various parts of which Clouston suggests supply all early Arabic prosodic terminology), often a feature of holidays, and several poets do holiday in my poem, as well as its speaker, and myself from my usual styles of writing poetry.

'The television and cocktail survives from Sam's poem into mine, as does its phrase "Romanian wannabe", but the "Grand Hotel Abyss" is from Lukács (deported to Romania after the fall of the 1956 Hungarian Revolution), his coinage for an imaginary salubrious holiday establishment, from the terraces of which the likes of Adorno enjoyed pessimistic views. Xavier de Maistre checks in to my poem later, whose '*Voyage autour de ma chambre*' lay behind de Selby's immobile holidays in *The Third Policeman*, as that book's boxes lie behind many of mine, from the TV I watch while writing (like Ashbery) to The Apocalypse's dimensions of the New Jerusalem invoked here and the melting ice cube of this poem's own end. Paradoxically, it all represents an attempt to think outside the box for me, and I'm grateful to the editors of *The Poetry Review* and this book for being interested in the result.'

JOE DUNTHORNE's debut novel, *Submarine*, was adapted for film by Richard Ayoade and translated into fifteen languages. His second, *Wild Abandon*, won the 2012 Encore Award. His stories and poems have been published in *The Paris Review*, *McSweeney's* and *London Review of Books*. His poetry pamphlet was published by Faber & Faber. He lives in London. Joe writes, 'On my computer, I have a folder labelled "recycle" which is full of phrases I've salvaged from otherwise disastrous poems. For a long time, I had the line "babies jangled down on their cords like oxygen masks". It kept migrating through different poems without ever finding a suitable home. At first, I kept trying to put it in funny poems because I thought it was a funny line but, as I got older, the line started to seem less and less funny and was not really funny at all by the time it appeared in this poem.'

FRANCINE ELENA was born in Canterbury in 1986 and grew up in London, Portugal, and Scotland, graduating from the University of Edinburgh with an MA in Classics. She works in publishing as an assistant editor. Her chapbook *Christmas Lantern* is published by 3:AM Press and her unpublished pamphlet *Fluoro* was shortlisted for the 2014 Poetry School Pighog Prize. Her poems have appeared in various publications including *The Best British Poetry 2013*, *The Sunday Times*, *Poetry London*, *The Quietus*, *Ambit*, *3:AM Magazine* and *Wasafiri*. She writes, 'This poem takes the idea of a long distance video call, communicated via references to works of art (and art within art and reinterpretations of art) that I love, like an image made of collaged images (and images within images) to make it more aesthetically beautiful and indirect. The title, "Fish Magic", is taken from the name of a painting by Paul Klee (1925), described on his website as "an inky black atmosphere of indeterminate scale and scope, where fish and flora float among human beings and clock towers". The opening lines of dialogue are taken from a conversation between the poet Matthew Gregory and the artist Marisa Argentato at the exhibition *Time to Rise* in May 2014, a show that explored the relationship between humans and technology, the organic and inorganic. There are references to Baz Luhrmann's 1996 version of *Romeo and Juliet* (1597), its fishtank with its song by Des'ree (that was adapted by Beyoncé and the subject of a lawsuit in 2007).

'The shape of the poem is inspired by ancient Greek concrete poems from around 300 BC. The first draft of "Fish Magic" was straight on one side, like Simias' "The Wings", then changed to the shape of Simias' "The Axe", similar to George Herbert's "Easter Wings" (1633). There is an echo in the shape of Juliet's wings, of fish tails, of an hourglass and two heads either side. While the song "Kissing You" is about being apart, the poem within *Kuruntokai* (6/7 CE) is about two people coming closer together. Each poem I write inexplicably takes on a colour in my mind's eye and "Fish Magic" is hot pink.'

INUA ELLAMS, born in Nigeria, is a cross art form practitioner, a poet, playwright and performer, a graphic artist and designer. He is a Complete Works poet alumnus, currently a playwright-in-resident at Soho Theatre, resident at the Southbank Centre's Poetry Library and a graphic designer at White Space Creative Agency. Across his work, Identity, Displacement and Destiny are recurring themes in which he also tries to mix the old with the new: traditional African storytelling with contemporary poetics / pencil with pixel / texture with vector images. His pamphlets of poetry are published by Flipped Eye and Akashic Books and several plays by Oberon. He comments, 'I had the title "Swallow Twice" before I had the poem. I have fifty-five such titles and nine-ish poems written. These poems will make up my first full collection, which will be called *Of All The Boys Of Plateau Private School* (which is also a poem published in *Best British Poetry 2011*). The idea was a naively simple one: to explode a poem; to carve its lines into groups of words, use as titles for my first collection and write chronologically from childhood into adulthood. The first difficulty was and has been finding ideas for poems that do the titles justice enough and second is doing so whilst ensuring there are thematic and narrative arcs. I find myself writing and rewriting poems and sometimes, the rewrites are entirely different, such that I have two existing poems titled "Swallow Twice", both of which have been published.

'This particular story was absorbed from my cousin, which is to say it didn't happen to me. My father told it so often, I began dreaming it as its protagonist and the poem came in one sitting, the editing, in a class run by Mimi Khalvati. It has been published in The Complete Works' *Ten* anthology, edited by Karen McCarthy Woolf, and in a recent pamphlet of poems, *The Wire-Headed Heathen*, published by Akashic Books, edited by Kwame Dawes and Chris Abani. I may *Swallow Twice* a third time.'

ANDREW ELLIOTT's collection *Mortality Rate* is published by CBeditions.

VICTORIA FIELD was born in London in 1963. She works as a writer and poetry therapist and is now based in Canterbury after many years in Cornwall and, previously, Russia, Turkey and Pakistan. Her third collection *The Lost Boys* (Waterloo, 2013) won the Holyer an Gof Award for poetry and drama. Her plays have been performed at Hall for Cornwall and the Marlowe Studio and she is a former writer-in-residence at Truro Cathedral. She has co-edited three books on therapeutic writing and is a member of the British Psychological Society. She writes, 'They say the past is another country and I think that particularly applies to the 1970s, the decade of my teenage years. I grew up in a small village and attended a girls' grammar school in a nearby market town. The school was old-fashioned even then and the market town, dreary. The countryside though was beautiful and I roamed on foot and on my bicycle enjoying a freedom unthinkable today. The public library introduced me to wider worlds and as soon as I was seventeen, the minimum age for being an au pair in Belgium, I escaped abroad and lived adventurously until returning to Kent a few years ago.

'Coming back to the area after such a long gap has been a trigger for memories. Once I started thinking about my school days, poems began suggesting themselves as accounts of small epiphanies, such as the day when Mrs Bagnall really did explain magnesium. To my surprise, I find I learned more than I thought at the school I couldn't wait to leave. In the spirit of writing letters to the dead, I want to name those teachers in that other country and acknowledge the various gifts I received from them.'

ANNIE FREUD is a poet and artist. Her first collection was *A Voids Officer Achieves the Tree Pose*, a pamphlet published by Donut Press in 2007. Her first full collection, *The Best Man That Ever Was* (Picador, 2007) was a Poetry Book Society Recommendation and was awarded The Dimplex Prize for New Writing (Poetry section). *The Mirabelles* (Picador, 2010), her second collection, was a Poetry Book Society Choice and was short-listed for the T.S. Eliot Prize. She has been named by the Poetry Book Society as one of the Next Generation Poets 2014. Her third collection, *The Remains*, was published in June 2015 and is a Poetry Book Society Recommendation. Her poems have appeared in many magazines, anthologies and websites. She has taught poetry composition for many years and is renowned for her live performances. Annie notes, 'When I think about an important relationship, the aspect that perhaps matters to me most are the words that the person in question has said to me over the course of a lifetime, that have left an indelible memory and that stand as a reminder of what made them unique.

'The words in this poem were once said to me by my father. At the time I remember thinking that there were many possible answers that I could have made to that statement, but that none of them seemed adequate and so I stayed silent. The *not* giving voice to these connotations is essential to the poem.

'In a way these words embody the way he lived his life. I remember several times during my youth being taken by him to a maternity ward to see a newborn baby whom he had fathered, although nothing whatsoever was said about that, and the intense sense of satisfaction that he radiated. But it is so much more than that.

'I love the thought that control is something to be enjoyed. It is exciting to think that by concentrating and focusing on one's intentions and desires, something extraordinary can be released.'

MATTHEW GREGORY was born in Suffolk, in 1984. His poems have appeared in magazines and anthologies since 2005 and he has collaborated with artists in Naples, Berlin and Frankfurt on installations and film. He received an Eric Gregory award in 2010 and a Hawthornden Fellowship in 2014. He notes, '"Decline of the House" (House of Bourbon, at Versailles) was sewn together from the salvaged parts of other poems. Because of that, it has a reverse chronology, as far as history is concerned: Madame de Tourzel died in the 19th century, the second section refers to Louis XVI, the third to the Sun King. As the poem itself is comprised of this essential fracture, linear time is suspended or disassembled, something that appealed to my understanding of the decline of Versailles, which is that it can be detected in its beginning. Where else were all those rococo swirls heading, if not into a vortex?'

DAVID HART writes, 'I recall seeing a poem in print attached to my name and feeling sure there had been some mistake, having no memory of it. I had to check through my files, and did find it. "He wrote" is one I recognise as mine, while having no recollection of how it came to be written. I see that it begins with my being now (in Birmingham) "of a good age" (if indeed "He" is precisely me) and it arrives back at my life as a choirboy in Aberystwyth. "God be in my head" does now need scratching. I am surprised the middle of the poem features no hut, way out there in that no-place place. Something oddly true can occur, can't it, if one is dropped out of the daily air into a flow-spin.

'After some forty-five years in Birmingham my imagination does still spring from my mid-Wales by the sea youth. I came to the city from London university and a curacy to be a university chaplain, since then was a theatre critic for the *Birmingham Post*, worked for the then West Midlands Arts for fifteen years, thereafter freelance, including hospital, festival and cathedral residencies, was the city's first selected Poet Laureate, poems widely published, books have included my Bardsey Island *Crag Inspector* (Five Seasons Press) and a new book – following my Birmingham new library attachment – *Library Inspector* (Nine Arches). And it pleases me greatly to be in this present book that includes a poem by my son Caleb.'

SELIMA HILL was born in 1945 into a family of painters. She read Moral Sciences at Cambridge and now lives by the sea in Dorset with her family and dogs. She writes, '"My Father's Smile" appears in *Jutland*, my thirteenth collection, a PBS Special Commendation, and shortlisted for the 2015 Roehampton Poetry Prize. The poem is from a sequence about my father, a subject that, until the deaths of my sisters, I had not felt free to address.'

SARAH HOWE was born in Hong Kong in 1983. Her first book, *Loop of Jade* (Chatto & Windus, 2015), was shortlisted for the Forward Prize for Best First Collection. Her tall-lighthouse pamphlet, *A Certain Chinese Encyclopedia*, won an Eric Gregory Award in 2010. Her work appears in *The Salt Book of Younger Poets* (Salt, 2011), *Dear World & Everyone In It* (Bloodaxe, 2013) and *Ten: The New Wave* (Bloodaxe, 2014). She is the founding editor of *Prac Crit*, an online journal of poetry and criticism. In 2015–16, she will be a Fellow at Harvard University's Radcliffe Institute. She writes, '"Sirens" comes from a sequence running through *Loop of Jade*, which steps back to offer an oblique and riddling perspective on some of the book's more straightforwardly "autobiographical" pieces. I wrote one poem for each of the creatures listed in the famous entry on "animals" from "a certain Chinese encyclopedia" the Argentine writer Jorge Luis Borges quoted (or rather invented) in one of his essays. Among this spuriously oriental work's peculiar categories, "sirens" rub shoulders with "stray dogs", "sucking pigs", "others", and beasts "that from a long way off look like flies". Borges's confection of wry Chinoiserie instantly spoke to me, as someone half-Chinese half-white, who felt vaguely monstrous as a child transplanted to England. "Sirens" kicks off the sequence's work of meditating on hybridity – creatures born between cultures, but also ones hovering across other sorts of binary: imagination and reality, angel and beast. The "pickerel-girl" flickers between opposed identities and interpellations, a bit like the perceptual conundrum of Wittgenstein's rabbit-duck.

'I'll mention one other provocation less evident than the chain of references embedded in the poem itself (whose musty, donnish tone I meant with a pinch of self-mockery!). "Sirens" bears the marks of my long fascination with a poem by Robert Hass called "Heroic Simile". Homeric-simile-cum-shaggy-dog-story, the poem's "punch-line" reveals its preceding, increasingly elaborate imaginative wanderings to be a sort of exercise in willed self-distraction. The last three lines unmask what's gone before as an effort to sublimate the erotic charge between two people who can't afford to acknowledge such undercurrents: "A man and a woman walk from the movies / to the house in the silence of separate fidelities. / There are limits to imagination."'

KATHLEEN JAMIE was born in the west of Scotland in 1962. Her poetry collections to date include *The Overhaul* (2012), which won the 2012 Costa Poetry Prize and *The Tree House*, which won both the Forward Prize and the Scottish Book of the Year Award. Kathleen Jamie also writes non-fiction including the highly regarded *Findings* and recently, *Sightlines*.

TOM JENKS has published three poetry collections with if p then q and a number of other books, the most recent being *1000 Proverbs* with S.J. Fowler (Knives Forks and Spoons), *The Tome of Commencement* (Stranger Press) and *Crabtree* (The Red Ceilings Press). He co-organises The Other Room reading series and website in Manchester, administers the avant objects imprint zimZalla and is a PhD student at Edge Hill University. He comments, '*Spruce* in its complete form is a ninety-part poem, with each part comprising three stanzas of three lines each. It incorporates some fragments of found text, but in the main was written rapidly in longhand on lunch breaks, on public transport and in various provincial shopping malls and melancholic chain hotels in David Cameron's Britain. The focus of *Spruce* is temporal rather than thematic, with the parts serving as oblique records of what it was to be in particular places at particular times, reading particular free newspapers and thinking particular thoughts, with minimal editing. It does not aim to say anything in particular, but nor does it seek to avoid saying. *Spruce* unashamedly privileges the ephemeral over the eternal and surface over depth. It can be described as a poem of the long now, where everything that happens and has happened happens at once, where King John and Lenin occupy the same space as Piers Morgan and the cast of *Glee*. The milieu of the poem is mainly urban, although there are flowers, grass and trees if you look for them, usually growing on a mini-roundabout. If I was making grand claims, I'd call it a business park pastoral or a sustained work of muffled hysteria, like someone screaming under a duvet.'

LUKE KENNARD is the author of four collections of poetry. He won an Eric Gregory Award from the Society of Authors in 2005 for his first collection of prose poems *The Solex Brothers*. His second, *The Harbour Beyond the Movie*, was shortlisted for the Forward Prize for Best Collection in 2007, making him the youngest writer ever to be shortlisted. He has a PhD in English from the University of Exeter and lectures at the University of Birmingham. In 2014 he was named one of the Next Generation Poets by the Poetry Book Society in their once-per-decade list. He writes, 'Cain had been cropping up in scraps and drafts for a year before I decided to actually start researching him. So much has been written about the first murderer, from Rabbinical dialogues to early church theologians to long poems by Byron and Coleridge (with approx. 1,400 critical commentaries on those poems) that I quickly found I was able to replace the frustrating and painful writing process with just reading and making notes: a happy time. Then I met the Canadian poet Gregory Betts and he gave me his book *If Language*, which uses the long perfect anagram on a critical passage. I was entranced by the idea, and Betts told me a little about the anagram's role in Jewish mysticism, which made it seem doubly relevant to the Cain project. One of the reasons I chose this passage from the King James Version is that it concerns the ground itself being cursed. I wanted to see what new variations could be "grown" from the words. I decided I needed a loose sense of plot, that it should be a kind of "flatshare comedy". The sequence gradually developed into a story where Cain and Father K. are trying to smuggle their friend Adah across the border, and the 31 anagrams will form the middle section of my next book, *Like Cain*, sandwiched between two less opaque sequences (although all the poems are about me and Cain and the overall book will explore one story). There's a preponderance of "h"s in the KJV, so I often got about 80% through an anagram to realise that I had 23 left over and that I would have to start again and try to use words with more "h"s from the start. There's an unavoidable essence of the OuLiPo whenever you use a technique like this, something which foregrounds a love of linguistic games, and the dramaticule deliberately echoes Alfred Jarry's *Ubu* trilogy (which I hate, by the way).'

AMY KEY's debut collection *Luxe* was published by Salt in 2013. She is editor of *Best Friends Forever* – poems on female friendship (The Emma Press, 2014) and founder and co-editor of online journal *Poems in Which*. She writes, 'Because the poem discloses something that has been so damaging to me I don't feel able to judge its value. In my heart I think it might be a *bad* poem. Nonetheless, I needed to say something and it came out this way. It being published helped to overcome a little of the shamefulness I carry with me, and some other women wrote to me to say they had found it helpful in regard to their own experiences – for that I am grateful.'

KATE KILALEA moved to London in 2005 to study for her MA in Creative Writing at the University of East Anglia. Her first book of poetry, *One Eye'd Leigh* (Carcanet, 2009) was shortlisted for the Costa Poetry Award and longlisted for the Dylan Thomas Prize for writers under 30. She comments, 'I always introduce this poem, and the sequence to which it belongs, by describing their setting, which is an imaginary building called The House for the Study of Water. The House for the Study of Water is inspired by the glass buildings designed by the architect Bruno Taut in his book *Alpine Architecture*. Most of the poems in the sequence, including this one, take the form of letters written from a man living in the House for the Study of Water to his brother, Max. His letters, on the whole, are preoccupied with the natural world – the landscape and animals – which is perhaps what one would expect from a man living on his own in a glass-walled house. Using transparent walls, according to Taut, would bring a house's inhabitants closer to nature. But what is closeness? What does it mean to be intimate with nature? And what does it mean, for a person living in a glass house, to be so constantly exposed?

'On another note, it may be of interest to anyone as attracted to dogs as I am to Google "Kafka + dog-like" or "Deleuze + write like a dog", neither of which have any bearing on the poem.'

CALEB KLACES' *Bottled Air* won the Melita Hume Prize for Best First Collection and an Eric Gregory Award. He has written poems, essays and stories for magazines including *Poetry*, *Granta*, *The Threepenny Review*, *Boston Review*, *The White Review*, *Conjunctions* and the *LRB* blog, and performed at festivals including Aldeburgh, The Maastricht International Poetry Nights and the BBC Proms. Caleb comments as follows, 'I applied for some money to write poems as annotations to the very short 1933 correspondence between Albert Einstein and Sigmund Freud, in which Einstein asked Freud how people can stop one another warring, and Freud told Einstein people can't. When I received the funds I realised my idea was not good. I wrote twenty-three sex sonnets instead. A year later I liked lots of the parts of what I had written but didn't like the whole. I was annoyed at how balanced the sonnets were, so I tested out forms which emphasise imbalance. I had the feeling that all the lines of all the sonnets were too far away from one another, so I tried to get them to interfere and touch. I tripped over, got ahead of, aroused and repeated myself, but came up against the problem that words have to be read one at a time. I compromised by starting new sentences before previous ones have finished. I have a document of parts of sonnets that didn't make it into 'Genit—'. There are two lines in that document which I still like: "It is a source of amusement to me how those who don't believe / your theories use your words." I don't know where they belong.'

ZAFFAR KUNIAL was born in Birmingham and now lives in Manchester, having moved from Cumbria where he was the Wordsworth Trust Poet in Residence. His poem 'The Word' was recently chosen for the Geoffrey Dearmer Prize by judge Bill Manhire. Zaffar's pamphlet *Faber New Poets 11* was published in 2014. He comments, 'That phrase my dad coined, *enjoy the life*, haunted me – along with a kind of attached shame – and I suppose I was just exploring that. I can still see him standing in the doorway. I didn't know "The Word" would end how it did, but its last line came in the first draft. It took a while for the poem to find its shape. I remember editing it one night in a place called Fanny's Ale House in Saltaire and the shape came then. I like how the poem looks a bit like a door. My dad wasn't schooled beyond the age of seven and he said he taught himself to read English from looking at shop signs, and he'd worked in a factory most of his time over here – and I felt misunderstood and ashamed on a few levels at the position I was in. I suppose, looking back, I may have been writing about positioning; how the positioning of words can lock them in the memory, even when they seem "wrong". I was thinking about other things too, which is why I called it "The Word", partly to link to that biblical phrase "In the beginning was the Word". I did spend one summer holiday not wanting to go out, and mostly in my bedroom and it wasn't like him to knock on the door like that.'

DAISY LAFARGE was born in Hastings and will graduate from the University of Edinburgh in 2016. Her writing has appeared in print and online in publications such as *Galavant, clinic* and *The Quietus*. She remarks, 'A few months after writing the poem – stitched together from a series of observations and experiences, fruitlessly wondering whether observation is collapsed complicity – I was reading R.D. Laing differentiating between behaviour and experience. Each person's experience is unique to them, but experienced by others as behaviour, which stands in for their experience, and so on . . .

'"I do not experience your experience. But I experience you as experiencing. I experience myself as experienced by you. And I experience you as experiencing yourself as experienced by me."* Reclining with the contradictions, conflicts and misunderstandings of experience and behaviour is perhaps the best position from which to read the poem. It became a record – as well as an example itself – of these contradictions: feeling in and outside of certain situations or structures at the same time; the way certain ideologies – unwelcome and otherwise – take root in your behaviour and thought process. The writing became a bit like an exorcism of these, but perhaps only half of one. A total exorcism would be too hopeful and holistic an ambition. (*The Politics of Experience,* 1967)'

MELISSA LEE-Houghton is a Next Generation Poet 2014. Her two collections, *A Body Made of You* and *Beautiful Girls* are published by Penned in the Margins. *Beautiful Girls* was a PBS Recommendation. Previous to these was a book-length poem, *Patterns of Mourning*, published by Chipmunka. Her work has been broadcast on BBC Radio Four and a full recording of her work features on The Poetry Archive online. Her third collection is forthcoming. She writes, 'It's true that I never set out to write this poem. It's also true that when it was written I was afraid of it. I thought I might never show it to another person, but it is now out there in the big, bad world. Death and sex are related in the sense that we should approach them both with excited terror and they both bring home to us our existential reality: we are all alone, but in desire and in love we can experience belonging, synchronicity and a temporary wane in our sense of loneliness-in-the-world. I think desire is often a sticking point in society, even in art; we are suspicious of it, we are afraid of it and very often the discussions surrounding it are volatile and unbalanced. I find BDSM-related conversations can be isolating in their two-sidedness and there is very little real discussion on, for example, how people can repair after sexual abuse and what role sex can play in a life tainted by sexual violence. I think of our emotional and inner lives as spectrums of colour and unique complexity; I think of my poetry as trying to express in words this myriad – in my own world at least – not just as autobiography but as art. I allow myself to feel, to assert my restless thoughts and impulses on the page to fight back against all that taught me to stay still and silent, and I write in the hope of the possibility it may also allow others a voice.'

DOROTHY LEHANE is a PhD candidate in Poetry at the University of Kent. Her research explores the perceptual and social experiences of neurological speech conditions, and examines questions concerning cultural encounters and embodied responses within representational poetic practice. She is the author of *Ephemeris* (Nine Arches Press, 2014) and *Places of Articulation* (dancing girl press 2014). She is the founding editor of Litmus Publishing, and teaches Creative Writing at the University of Kent. She comments, 'It is possible that there is a link between the observance of the rules of the universe, and closed poetic patterns. Order and symmetry is often purposefully recreated in poetic work. Traditional forms and conventions are often found in cosmological poetry; lyrical verses which use meter, repetition, and rhyme to communicate reveries on the beauty, majesty and the larger concepts of the Universe. This poem was part of a larger project engaging with cosmological phenomena. Rather than finding the Universe ordered, I found much of the theory chaotic, that the poetic techniques of collage and non sequitur lent themselves to the plethora of scientific theories. The Universe itself could never be neatly encapsulated, with its fracture and fragmented theory. I began to feel quite connected to the disarray and my poetic rhythm, language, and syntax began to align with the disorder. We strive to tune out background noise, the cosmic background radiation that permeates our Universe; the hiss which can be seen or heard when we detune a TV or radio in order to focus entirely on one stream of noise. Much of the language I used seemed to be born from this background echo, an undertow permeating my work with force and rhythm.'

FRAN LOCK is the author of two collections, *Flatrock* (Little Episodes, 2011), and *The Mystic and The Pig Thief* (Salt, 2014). She is the Winner of the 2014 Ambit Poetry Competition, and her poem 'Last Exit to Luton' won third prize in the Poetry Society's National Poetry Competition 2014. Fran comments, '"Melpomene" is one poem in a series of nine that recasts the Greek *Mousai* as modern traveller women. When I began researching the Muses I became interested in how their roles had been tailored and shaped over time to serve the private peccadillos of artists or the hidden agendas of culture. I wanted to write something that showed how these women might work with and against the taboos, prejudices and stereotypes they'd been branded with; the way they use or subvert them to create and recreate themselves. I was thinking in particular about "otherness" and how it operates, how it affects people, particularly women. To be "gypsy" is to be an object of both fantasy and scorn. I'm interested in that contradiction, that hypocrisy, and what it does to the people who have to live with and within it. Melpomene is the Muse of Tragedy. The poem's speaker carries the inherited tragedies of her people, but also the miseries of imperfect assimilation. This is theme I return to again and again in my work.'

ADAM LOWE is an award-winning writer, publisher and creative producer from Leeds, who now lives in Manchester. He performs live art and cabaret as Beyonce Holes. He has appeared in such anthologies and magazines as *The Sunday Telegraph, Ten: The New Wave, Black & Gay in the UK, The Cadaverine, The Nervous Breakdown* and *Word Riot*. In 2014 he produced a one-man show, *Ecstasies* (directed by Gerry Potter), for Queer Contact festival, which toured Manchester, Leeds and Brighton, and performed at events as diverse as Queer Contact, Polari Literary Salon, Nine Worlds GeekFest, Sparkle transgender festival, Cha Cha Boudoir and PoMoGaze (University of Leeds). In the same year he coordinated the Young Enigma Awards 2014, and produced and performed in *Patterflash!*, a 'literary variety show' which ran during Edinburgh Fringe to full audiences every night. He explains, 'The poem is written in Polari, a kind of gay slang that emerged from the secret codewords of the theatre and prostitutes (West End girls) and cockney rhyming slang, Yiddish and thieves' cant (East End boys). It was popularised on the radio show *Round the Horne*, but shortly afterwards fell into disuse, as men who have sex with men no longer needed to disguise their words. But in recent years, the language has gained a new respect, and has begun to be used again. The poem is a celebration of that.'

CHRIS MCCABE's collections are *The Hutton Inquiry, Zeppelins, THE RESTRUCTURE* and, most recently, *Speculatrix*. He has recorded a CD with the Poetry Archive and was shortlisted for the Ted Hughes Award in 2014. His plays *Shad Thames, Broken Wharf* and *Mudflats* have been performed in London and Liverpool and his prose book *In the Catacombs: A Summer Among the Dead Poets of West Norwood Cemetery* was a London Review of Books Bookshop title of the year. With Victoria Bean he has just co-edited *The New Concrete: Visual Poetry in the 21st Century*, which is available from Hayward Publishing. Chris comments, 'I wrote this poem in my mum's old house, a few years after my dad died; the house I grew up in, just before it had to be sold. I'd just moved house myself and as I didn't yet have an internet connection I took my laptop to my mum's so I could do some work. As I arrived I realised there was a man in a suit sitting on the sofa my dad used to sit on, evaluating the cost of the house that my dad had worked all of his life to pay for. I had a very primitive reaction to the situation, to the clean, cold way in which the man from the estate agent could map the house I'd grown up in to the local markets. After he left my mum went out for a while and I was alone in the house, aware that this would probably be the last time that I'd be there. I walked around looking at things: the stained-glass window in the hall (the way it cast a sepia yellow light on the stairs – a memory before language) and a sequence of images from the past came back: how the cats used to play in an old bath in the snow, how my younger brother and I used to pause cartoons and draw them from stills, how we used to make stink bombs and put them under each other's beds. I wrote the first draft of the poem there and then. Sometimes I've felt that poetry serves a role for me in addressing a crisis before it becomes fact, allowing me to thrash it out on my own terms. A few weeks later the house was on the market and quickly sold.'

AMY MCCAULEY has recently completed a collection of poems (*Auto-Oedipa*) which re-imagines the Oedipus myth. Her new project is a verse-novel about the life of Joan of Arc, an extract of which was longlisted for the KCL Responses to Modernism Prize 2015. Amy is also writing a book of essays under the pseudonym 'Kathy Groan' and a new stage play. She is poetry submissions editor for *New Welsh Review*. She writes, '*Old habits die hard and language is an old habit. Poetry, too, is an old habit.* Every speech-form, even the unusual or isolated, can be seen not only as a testimony to the man who coined it, but also as a document in the life of the language, and evidence of its possibilities at a given time.'[1]

'*"Kadmea Touch Me" might be called a many-mouthed incident. A many-mouthed incident is perilous in ways a "poem" is not. I propose that peril is necessary for the survival of the artist.*

'[c]ritics have been slow to realize that literature, being based on language, cannot [. . .] get at the things behind language in some special way and that there may, in fact, be nothing (at least for the human mind) more real than forms of language.'[2]

'*Utterance is an instrument of violence. "Voice" is not an expression of personality but a genealogy of sound effects.*

'Isn't it that one wants to be as factual as possible and at the same time as deeply suggestive or deeply unlocking of areas of sensation other than simple illustration of the object that you set out to do? Isn't that what all art is about?[3]

'*Art is revolutionary only if it understands that the idea of revolution is contingent on our understanding of its antithesis.*'

[1] Benjamin, W., *The Origin of German Tragic Drama* (London: Verso, 2009), p. 49.

[2] Forrest-Thomson, V., *Poetic Artifice* (Manchester: Manchester University Press, 1978), p. 28.

[3] Bacon, F., interview with David Sylvester, published as *Interviews with Francis Bacon* (London: Thames and Hudson, 1975), p. 56.

ALEX MACDONALD lives and works in London. His poetry has been published in *Poetry London*, *Poetry Wales*, *The Rialto*, *3:AM* and *The Quietus*. He was the Digital Poet in Residence for the Poetry School and he hosted 'Selected Poems at the V&A Reading Rooms' which celebrated independent poetry presses and the poets they publish. He is one of the editors of the online poetry magazine *Poems in Which*. He comments, '"End Space" is the longest poem I've written and it was also the first poem I was commissioned to write. The Lion and Lamb Gallery in London asked me to respond to their exhibition focusing on the theme of "Rest". I took the artist Freyja Wright's painting *Interior Sequence* as my starting point – a diptych showing a reflection of a silhouetted woman. In the first painting she is looking out of a bright window, in the second she is looking away from it.

'There was an isolated quietness in these paintings. Just before writing the poem, I was in Berlin and did a lot of walking. I went to Potsdam just outside the city and visited the Albert Einstein Science Park which was filled with austere and impressive buildings, including the tower that was built for the namesake physicist to test his theory of general relativity. I'm not much of a science buff but the empty roads and walkways for the scientists, busy at work in their buildings, had this unsettling feeling. This put me in the mind of the large Victorian asylums throughout England and, ultimately, the idea of a "rest cure". Other sights in Berlin feature in the poem, except the hospital beds by the sea, which I saw in Berck, a French seaside town. Strangely, there wasn't anyone on the beach that day.

'The title is not mine – it's from the collection of architectural drawings by Daniel Libeskind. These drawings are completely manic, often looking like a building mid-explosion. They are architecturally impossible.'

ANDREW MCMILLAN was born in South Yorkshire in 1988; his first collection *physical*, published by Jonathan Cape in July 2015, was a Poetry Book Society Recommendation for Autumn 2015 and shortlisted for the Forward Prize for Best First Collection as well as being longlisted for the Guardian First Book Award. He currently lectures in Creative Writing at Liverpool John Moores University. He remarks, 'This poem came out of a great Viking poetry project, run by Dr Debbie Potts; a few contemporary poets were asked to "translate", or interpret, some Skaldic verse – I was given the poet Egill Skallagrímsson; Debbie provided a literal translation into modern English and also lots of background notes and ideas about certain words – in many ways she deserves all the credit. I tried to keep some of the original feel of the poem, whilst also taking in other things that were on my mind at the time; I'd spoken with poet Alicia Stubbersfield about the anxieties of masculinity in men who were born in the generation after the Second World War, and I'd been reading Lachlan Mackinnon's great prose poem, "The Book of Emma", which has some wonderful parts about Hemingway. These two things came together with the violence and anger that seemed to run through the original verses. The squashedupwords are a feature of much of my poetry, and could be seen as a modern version of the kenning. Possibly. Really this poem belongs to two other people, Egill and Debbie; it's not mine. And now it's yours.'

KATHRYN MARIS's second collection, *God Loves You*, was published by Seren in 2013. Her poems have appeared in *Best British Poetry 2012*, *The Pushcart Prize Anthology* and many periodicals in the US and the UK. She teaches for the Poetry School in London and the Arvon Foundation. She writes, 'This poem's genre and style could be described, respectively, as "science fiction" and "effortfully unmusical". I've written other poems in this pseudoscientific vein, poems with an unspecified narrator that might be an anthropologist or computer from the future whose knowledge of our era is simultaneously accurate and false.

'For me, the appealing part of this poem's origin story is what happened after *Granta* accepted it. Poetry Editor Rachael Allen was like a friendly drill sergeant. She suggested I remove the ampersands in favour of the word "and"; she merged some sentences and separated others; and she asked me to rethink my original compound noun "wishing well" in line four because she felt it didn't have a scientific enough register. She was right on all counts.

'I then sent my poem to the physicist and writer Frank Close and asked if he could think of a scientific alternative to "wishing well", perhaps one related to particle physics. He suggested "linear collider", "cyclotron", "cavity resonator", "integrated circuit" and other possibilities, admitting that none were especially poetic. Meanwhile I had come across the term "potential well" which, I believe, has something to do with energy. I wrote a second email to Frank: "What do you think about a 'potential well'?" His response was, "Well, that has potential!"

'Rachael, too, liked the suggestion. But because our well was unique and imaginary we turned it into a proper noun: Potential Well.

'I say *our* well because the poem – despite its private beginnings as a dream filtered through my obsession with medical topics including the microbiome – was, ultimately, a collaboration.'

SOPHIE MAYER is a writer, editor and educator. With Markie Burnhope and Sarah Crewe, she edited *Catechism: Poems for Pussy Riot* (English PEN, 2012), kicking off a wave of poetry activism that continued with *Binders Full of Women*, *Fit to Work: Poets against Atos* and *Against Rape*.

(O) (Arc, 2015) follows on from the feminist re-visioning of the Bible in her collaboration with Sarah Crewe, *signs of the sistership* (KFS, 2013), and from her solo collections *The Private Parts of Girls* (Salt, 2011) and *Her Various Scalpels* (Shearsman, 2009). She reviews poetry for *Shearsman Review*, and film for *Sight & Sound* and *The F-Word*. She writes as follows, 'This is a poem about not swallowing: about choking on, and being choked by, the patriarchal language and narrative of the state, organised religion, classical and canonical literature, the military, myth, marriage, family. It's about what happens when you choke, at the edge of breath and speech. What gets thrown up. To essay is to try, and in its experiment with form it reflects (on) the admixture of lyric, long poems, translations, and review essays that makes *The Wolf*, where it was published, unique.

'If the poem is an essay, it is so between the ways in which Anne Carson's poem "Essay on What I Think Most" and her critical piece "The Gender of Sound" are essays: prose fragments spoken in catches of breath. The paragraphs act like messages on a postcard, sent from Aulis, where Iphigenia went first to swallow her marriage, then her death. It's part of a long history of speaking back to canonical texts; not least in recognising where those texts speak back to themselves, however elliptically or unconsciously, and however much they foreclose it punitively, through insurgent figures such as Iphigenia and Bathsheba.

'Dean Rader coins the phrase "the epic lyric" to describe the expansive compression of contemporary North American indigenous poetics, and I have learned from the approach of writers such as Allison Hedge Coke: "Silence, Singing" moves over millennia, from Biblical and Homeric events to the present, through their recounting, and re-counts their gendered cost. Both epic and lyric have been complicit in this (as they have in the framing of colonialism); working together – pulling against each other – the forms might offer a way out, as does the paradox heard in Iphigenia's silence, singing.'

KIM MOORE's first pamphlet *If We Could Speak Like Wolves* was a winner in the 2012 Poetry Business Pamphlet Competition and was shortlisted for a Michael Marks Award. Her first full-length collection *The Art of Falling* was published by Seren in 2015. She won the Geoffrey Dearmer Prize in 2010, an Eric Gregory Award in 2011 and a New Writing North Award in 2014. She works part-time as a peripatetic brass teacher. She writes, '"The Knowing" is from a sequence of poems called *How I Abandoned My Body To His Keeping*. The sequence explores domestic violence within a relationship. There are seventeen poems altogether and this is the sixth one in the sequence. Throughout the sequence I use animals and birds as a way of writing about trauma. The raven makes an appearance in a few of the other poems as well. I wanted to write about the different ways we have of knowing things – especially when dealing with difficult and painful subjects. The raven knows everything but remembers nothing and represents one tried and tested way of coping with trauma, but the poem tells you that the trees are the important thing. They are the witnesses to violence but they don't have a voice. However, the narrator of this poem is unreliable at best. How can you trust any poem that starts "The story goes"?'

SALAH NIAZI is an Iraqi poet: one of the pioneers of modern Arabic poetry. Exiled in 1964, he worked as newsreader, and Head of the Cultural Talks Unit at the BBC Arabic Service for almost two decades, during which time he completed a PhD at the University of London. Dr Niazi has published many works of literature, including nine collections of poetry and six books of criticism. He has also published translations (into Arabic) of three Shakespeare plays, and Joyce's *Ulysses*. He writes, 'Every twist and turn in this poem is, simply, real. Yet, hopefully, it is neither vignette nor biographical. The late Shafiq Al-Kamali (to give him his full name) was a minister, a political leader, and a poet of a sort. We met once in Baghdad, and twice in London and Manchester where he had been invited by the Iraqi community to give poetry recitals. Our friendship was skin deep, did not go beyond that. There was not the remotest possibility to write anything, let alone an elegy, on him. But his death, or rather the mystery which wrapped round his death, gave way to sinister rumours telling the most horrendous story, about how he was torn to pieces. Then coincidentally, the country itself was in real turmoil which allowed fear to get hold of people. They were frightened but did not know what they were frightened of. Before writing this poem, I was for months nagged by three concepts: the frailty of man, despite an otherwise, strong façade (e.g. boxers); crime and punishment (e.g. the scales of Justine); and life's inevitable illusions. Are these part and parcel of our existence? But I must admit that none of these themes had anything to do with Kamali. How, then, did he sneak into the poem? I do not know. It may be one of the mysteries of making verses, or perhaps one of the tricks of the subconscious, or *quién sabe . . .* '

JEREMY OVER lives near Cockermouth in Cumbria. His poetry first appeared in the anthology *New Poetries II* (Carcanet, 1999) and his first two collections were *A Little Bit of Bread and No Cheese* (Carcanet, 2001) and *Deceiving Wild Creatures* (Carcanet, 2009). He is currently completing a third and studying for a PhD in Creative Writing at the University of Birmingham. He comments, '"Artificially Arranged Scenes" has existed in various different forms in my compost heap for over a decade. At one point it was entitled, "Scenes from the cutting room floor of George Méliès" which describes it pretty accurately although the poem is not composed of outtakes, as such, but of snippets from some of his most famous films, cut and pasted into a new arrangement. The resulting collage is intended as a homage to Méliès' delirious anticipatory surrealism and, in particular, to his use of stop-motion photography. Paul Hammond suggests in the introduction to his book *Marvellous Méliès* – one of my main sources for the collage – that Méliès considered the cinema "as a medium animated by marvellous moments owing little allegiance to the banal narrative structures that hold them prisoner". Most of the poems I've written, including this one, also look to evade those kinds of prison guards and using a collage technique is one of my favourite ways of doing that. I like the way in which, with collage, you can sometimes just lay out the source material and, out of the corner of your eye as it were, spot words taking on a life of their own and being attracted to one another, "making love" even, as per André Breton's command, or at least enjoying a little unexpected frottage. I feel I could draw analogies between this way of writing and the Grimm tale about the Elves and the Shoemaker but I'd need better relations with narrative structures or at least a pair of elves. Maybe I'll just go to bed and see what happens. I'm the youngest of three brothers. Méliès was the son of a shoemaker.'

BOBBY PARKER is a self-taught writer and artist, born in 1982 in Worcestershire, England. *Blue Movie*, his first full-length poetry collection, is available from Nine Arches Press. He currently lives in London. Bobby comments as follows, 'Written sometime in late Spring 2014, "Thank You for Swallowing My Cum" is a controversial love poem, although it wasn't intended to be that way. An awkward celebration of an intimate sex act? Yes. A poem intended to outrage and upset? Definitely not. At the time of writing this piece my life had been turned upside down due to a marriage breakdown, homelessness, poor health and chronic drug addiction. I was truly lost. There were few poems written during this time, and what little I did write turned out to be rather bleak meditations on the banality and brutality of love, the fragility of relationships as I had experienced them. Then, after many years battling depression, anxiety and intense self-loathing, I was given the opportunity to celebrate my physical self for the first time, to embrace what was once anathema to me: my own nakedness. To joyfully submit my body to another and revel in the giddy aftermath. "Thank You for Swallowing My Cum" is a strange document from a wild and reckless time spent dancing madly through the sad world searching for my place in it. I'm still not sure I have found my place, but I found out who I am. My decision (and indeed the decision of the woman in the poem) to accept the generous offer for this poem to be included in such a prestigious anthology did not come easily (no pun intended). But here it is, and it is here because the feeling is as true now as it was then.'

Rebecca Perry's pamphlet, *little armoured*, was published by Seren in 2012. *Beauty/Beauty*, her first full collection, was published by Bloodaxe in January 2015 and is a Poetry Book Society Recommendation. Her work can be found at *The Quietus* and *B O D Y*. She co-edits the online journal *Poems in Which*. Rebecca comments, 'My poem was written as part of Crispin Best's For Every Year project (foreveryyear.eu), for the year 1776, which saw the birth of the French botanist and politician Charles-François Brisseau de Mirbel. Reading about him I saw a biographical note – 'In 1823 Mirbel married Lizinska Aimée Zoé Rue, a French painter of miniatures.' I became interested in Lizinska, who was much celebrated in her lifetime, instead. I was taken with the idea of a marriage between a man in love with plant life and a woman driven by the replication of tiny details.'

Holly Pester is a poet, critic and practice-based researcher. Her doctoral research at Birkbeck, University of London examined the poetics of noise and media, and sound-driven poetry. Her current research seeks to develop innovative practice-led research methodologies in relation to feminist archive theory. Her latest collection drew on forms of gossip and anecdote as archive research, published by Book Works, 2015. She is now Lecturer in Poetry and Performance at University of Essex. She writes, '"The man from Okay" is from a series of poems called "Jokes that don't translate". The poems in the series were all composed drawing on bad translations of jokes in non-English languages found online, in archives and libraries. This poem was first published in *The White Review* No. 13, March 2015.'

Heather Phillipson received an Eric Gregory Award in 2008, a Faber New Poets Award in 2009 and has published books with Faber & Faber, Penned in the Margins and Bloodaxe. She is also an internationally exhibiting artist; forthcoming and recent solo exhibitions include the Istanbul Biennial, Performa New York, Sheffield Doc Fest, Opening Times (otdac.org), Schirn Frankfurt, Serpentine Gallery, Tate Britain, Bunker259 (New York), BALTIC Centre for Contemporary Art, the ICA and a video commission for Channel 4 television. She is Writer in Residence at the Whitechapel Gallery, London, in 2015. She writes, 'This poem was commissioned as part of an artists' writing project, *Cadavere Quotidiano* (roughly: daily cadaver), and published online and, subsequently, in print (by X-TRA, Los Angeles). A group of artists were invited to contribute one text each, over a number of days, related to cadavers: obituaries, elegies, eulogies, epitaphs, expirations, cessations, disappearances, beheadings and defenestrations – of ideas, emotions, images and movements. "Guess what?" is, accordingly, littered with corpses of everyday consumption – food waste, dead animals, skin, teeth, fingernails, self-constructed identities and concepts, plus time- and muscle-wastage.'

PADRAIG REGAN is from Belfast where he is currently a postgraduate student at the Seamus Heaney Centre at Queen's University. His poems have been published in *Magma*, *Poetry Ireland Review* and *Poetry Review*. He was a recipient of an Eric Gregory Award in 2015. He comments, 'This poem began with the title; for a while I had been looking into Dutch paintings of the seventeenth century, and on Clara Peeters' Wikipedia page I found a reference to a painting sold by Christie's of London which the auction house had titled *Apples, Cherries, Apricots and other fruit in a Basket, with Pears, Plums, Robins, a Woodpecker, a Parrot and a Monkey Eating Nuts on a Table*. The poems which I was writing at the time made use of a long line and extended syntax, so the kind of convolution that results from the conventions around naming still-life paintings was immediately appealing.

'The painting shows a table with a large basket of fruit, a few dead birds and a monkey. There is something about the monkey's posture – its raised shoulders, how it holds its tail – which made me wonder if the monkey knew it was doing something it shouldn't by eating the walnuts. This led me to think that the monkey was in some way responsible for the deaths of the birds, and that the painting shows the aftermath of something quite violent.'

SAM RIVIERE is the author of *81 Austerities* (2012), *Standard Twin Fantasy* (2014), and *Kim Kardashian's Marriage* (2015). He notes the following, 'This poem was commissioned in response to "Germany divided: Baselitz and his generation", an exhibition of post-war German printmakers at the British Museum. The poem is modelled after an untitled self-portrait by A.R. Penck, which is made up of rows of black ink dots applied with a brush. The poem was written to fill a side of A5 paper with a 1cm margin, using Microsoft Word's default font (Calibri). I was paid £350 to write the poem.'

SOPHIE ROBINSON was born in 1985. She has a PhD in Poetic Practice from Royal Holloway. Her first collection, *a*, came out from Les Figues in 2009, and her second collection, *The Institute of Our Love in Disrepair*, was published by Bad Press in 2012. In 2011, she was the poet in residence at the Victoria and Albert Museum. She works as a lecturer in poetry at UEA.

JESSICA SCHOUELA was born in Montreal and is currently pursuing her MA at UCL in Art History. Her dissertation focuses on a series of documentary films made on Fogo Island, Newfoundland in 1967 as a part of the Challenge for Change project. She has been published by The Emma Press (forthcoming), *Metatron*, *The Quietus*, *Poems in Which*, and *Squawk Back*, amongst others. She writes a blog called *Cabbage Moths Lay Their Eggs On My Kale*. She writes, '"Poem In Which I Watch Jane Brakhage Give Birth" was written as a response one year after viewing experimental filmmaker Stan Brakhage's short film "Window Water Baby Moving" filmed in 1958 which documents the birth of his daughter, Myrrena. I had initially seen the film in a class at McGill University called Poetics of the Image. One year later, I was remembering my visceral response, my identification with Brakhage's wife, Jane, and a feeling of physical empathy. The silent film runs for thirteen minutes and gorgeously depicts Jane in the bath during labour and giving birth to the couple's first child. It narrates the event by way of a non-linear montage of (at times repeated) shots of primarily Jane, the bathtub water and the window in the bathroom of their home. The shots are often close ups or even extreme close ups of isolated parts of Jane's body: her nipple, her belly button, her vagina. There are a few counter shots of Stan, sometimes kissing Jane. The film is extremely graphic and extremely human and consistently demands of the viewer to feel human as well, both corporeally and emotionally.'

STEPHEN SEXTON lives in Belfast where he is studying for a PhD in Creative Writing at the Seamus Heaney Centre for Poetry. His pamphlet, *Oils*, published by The Emma Press in 2014, was the PBS Winter Pamphlet Choice. Poems have appeared in *Poetry London*, *Poetry Ireland*, and as part of the Lifeboat series of readings. Stephen comments, 'One morning a couple of years ago, someone said the last line of this poem (before it was a line in a poem) and it sort of stunned me. I thought it was one of the saddest things I'd ever heard. In whatever space one is taken aback to, and for whatever reason, the image of a grieving Popeye immediately appeared, Popeye being the only other speaker I figured could say it.

'The poem is largely based on the 1954 episode, "Bride and Gloom", though I suspect there are other scenes in other episodes I've forgotten about, such as the 1957 episode "Nearlyweds". A couple of lines are modelled rhythmically on the *Popeye* theme tune, but they may resemble more the Mexican Hat Dance, which is perhaps sadder still.'

PENELOPE SHUTTLE lives in Cornwall. Her pamphlet *In The Snowy Air* appeared from Templar in 2014. She has two forthcoming books: *Heath* (in collaboration with John Greening) will be published by Nine Arches Press in summer 2016; *Will You Walk a Little Faster* will appear from

Bloodaxe on her seventieth birthday in May 2017. Penelope is a tutor and mentor for the Arvon Foundation and for the Poetry School, and is a former Chair of Falmouth Poetry Group. She writes, '"O blinde Augen / blöde Herzen!" (O blind eyes / stupid heart) is sung by Iseult, in Wagner's *Tristan and Iseult.* My elegy poem "O blinde Augen" was written after I had made my mind up to stop writing elegies. So, never say never, I guess. This poem came along. It approaches bereavement from a time when a decade has passed since the actual loss. It tries to convey my longing to resume contact with the person who has gone. While in the process of redrafting the poem I heard the opera commentator on Radio 3 mention Iseult's aria; as this poem begins with and continues on via a sorrowing voice I felt I had been given my title by Radio 3, out of the aethyr* as it were. There are no coincidences, according to Jung, but, he says, there are synchronicities. This was one. When I'm writing many impulses and memories combine with the present and living moment to help me realise a poem. That is the backstory of "O blinde Augen". (*Aethyr is, I discover, not a valid scrabble word) . . . '

HANNAH SILVA is a Birmingham-based poet, playwright and performer. She won the Tinniswood Award for *Marathon Tales* (co-written with Colin Teevan for BBC Radio 3). Her latest performance piece, *Schlock!*, premiered at the Aldeburgh Poetry Festival and has toured widely, featuring at Flip 2015 in Brazil. Her first collection, *Forms of Protest*, is published by Penned in the Margins. www.hannahsilva.co.uk. Hannah writes, 'This extract comes from *The Kathy Doll*, a book-length sequence which was originally conceived as a performance entitled *Schlock!*. The project re-writes and plays with material from *Fifty Shades of Grey* and Kathy Acker's *In Memoriam to Identity*. I began by taking lines from *Fifty Shades of Grey* and replacing the words "submissive" with "mother" and "dominant" with "child". Other strategies included a word search for every instance of the word "pain" in each book. These writing methods transformed the themes and language of *Fifty Shades of Grey* into strange narratives such as that of a relationship between a mother and a child, which morphs into the relationship of a woman and her body and experience of cancer. The work is loosely structured around the events of the final years of Kathy Acker's life, particularly her actions following being diagnosed with breast cancer. Ultimately I wrote through my source materials to explore sex, disease, control and death, taking Kathy's name as subject.

'This extract comes towards the end of the sequence. It draws words and sounds from the synonyms of "submissive" that Grey offers Anna in *Fifty Shades of Grey*: "Tractable, compliant, pliant, amenable, passive, resigned, patient, docile, tame, subdued". It also re-visits a couple of lines that reoccur throughout the sequence. "How much pain are you willing to experience?" is a question drawn from the contract in *Fifty Shades of Grey* ("How much pain is the submissive willing to experience?") and "Hurt me baby, show me what love is" is a line from *In Memoriam to Identity*. It is one of the least "cut up" sections of the work, and explores my relationship with the Kathy of my imagination.

'*Schlock!* was commissioned by The Poetry Trust and premiered at the Aldeburgh Poetry Festival in 2014. It is supported by the Arts Council England and produced by Penned in the Margins. Further extracts from *The Kathy Doll* have appeared in *Poetry Wales* and *The Other Room Anthology 7.*'

MARCUS SLEASE was born in Portadown, N. Ireland and moved to Las Vegas at age twelve and became Mormon. He is no longer Mormon. Currently, he lives in the Public Lansbury Housing Estate in Poplar, East London. He has performed his work at various festivals and events, such as Soundeye in Cork, Ireland, the Carrboro Poetry Festival in North Carolina, the Prague Microfestival in Prague, the Arnolfini Gallery in Bristol, and the Parasol Unit, the Hardy Tree Gallery, Rich Mix, and Vogue Fabrics in London. His most recent books are *Rides* (Blart Press) and *Mu (so) Dream (window)* (Poor Claudia). He notes, '"Trying to define yourself is like trying to bite your own teeth," said Alan Watts. This poem agrees. This poem has a problem. It wants to be real. It realises it is not special. This poem has no destination. It wants to keep going. It wants to be like life: directionless. This poem wants to be bodily but not too defined. It wants a light touch. It wants to talk to you. It doesn't want to take a flight of fancy. This poem did not grow up with a silver spoon. Eileen Myles said: "Sometimes you have to slow down or speed up to fart. The revolution is still occurring in the body." This poem agrees. This poem is a nerve movie. This poem is just a poem.'

GRETA STODDART was born in Oxfordshire in 1966. Her first collection *At Home in the Dark* (Anvil) won the Geoffrey Faber Memorial Prize 2002 and her second, *Salvation Jane*, was shortlisted for the Costa Book Award 2008. Her third book is *Alive Alive O* (Bloodaxe, 2015). She lives in Devon and teaches for the Poetry School. She writes, '"Letter from Sido" is an imagined letter from Sidonie Colette (née Landoy) to her daughter, the French writer, Colette. Sido was a huge presence in Colette's life, and an influence the writer felt grew stronger as she herself grew older. She even suggests her mother – simple, direct, earthy, nature-loving with a kind of anti-philosophical stance – was the better writer. Many of the bits of news and observations I have taken from either the letters she wrote to her daughter or Colette's own memories of her mother. These have been taken from two books – *My Mother's House*, translated by Una Vincenzo

Troubridge and Enid McLeod (Penguin) and *Break of Day*, translated by Enid McLeod (Capuchin Classics). The poem is a mixture of lifted, reworded and made-up lines.

'What inspired me to write the poem was reading a letter in which Sido tells her daughter, who has been ill, that she can't come and visit because she needs to stay at home to watch the rare flowering of a cactus. Most children would have been hurt by being so supplanted in their mother's affections but Colette's response was unusual; she was proud to be the daughter of the woman who wrote that letter. Proud, I take it, to have come from a person whose love extended beyond her own children, to the world at large and its other, less protected inhabitants – a spider, a cat, a wounded caterpillar. Or, as Lisa Allardice puts it, "the wisdom of her lesson [is] that ultimately the tug of human attachments must give way to a greater solidarity with nature." It is her mother's close and real relationship to the earth, rather than to its people, which, far from being sentimental or delusional, does in fact feel incredibly affirmative.'

CHLOE STOPA-HUNT is a poet, editor and freelance critic. Formerly a Foyle Young Poet of the Year, *Mays Anthology* editor and Chair of the Oxford University Poetry Society, she received an Eric Gregory Award in 2014. She notes, '"The Leopard-God" has scant connection to the real world. I borrowed the name Nicholas from Nicholas Hughes (Ted Hughes' and Sylvia Plath's son, who died in 2009), because it felt like the right sort of name – a domestic name; a name tied to the world of poetry, a sad name; and the name of St Nicholas, too – but the poem is certainly not "about" Nicholas Hughes in any direct sense. Many of my poems from recent years exist in a semi-dreamscape; not influenced by my own literal dreams, but dreamlike: surreal and image-driven like a dream. This poem is one of them. Owing to poor health and long periods of being housebound or bedbound, I often write about images and ideas which seem to come from my own mind (although who can say what is being refracted there?), since my real life involves no encounters or new experiences. No matter how unsatisfactory it may sound to admit that the god in this poem is no particular god, that is the truth. Yet I enjoyed telling the story for its own sake.'

REBECCA TAMÁS was born in London, and is currently studying for a PhD in Creative and Critical Writing at the University of East Anglia, where she is focusing on witchcraft, female alterity and ecopoetics. Her pamphlet, *The Ophelia Letters*, came out from Salt in 2013, and was short-listed for Best Poetry Pamphlet in the Saboteur Awards. She has work forthcoming in *para-text* and *The White Review*. She can be found online at @RebTamas. Rebecca comments, 'This poem is part of a series (still unfinished if I'm being honest) called *Extinct Species of the British Isles*. The aim was to write a poem titled with the name of each species that has become extinct throughout our history, and the year in which each extinction took place. The desire to do this was of course in some part ecological, hoping to draw attention to what has been lost so far, and what may be lost in the future. However, I didn't want the poems to simply be *about* the extinct animals, claiming a knowledge of the nonhuman for myself that would be utterly false, but, if possible, to imaginatively work alongside them, with them. I was curious to see what would happen when very human poems about personal experience rubbed up against the memory of these alien nonhuman creatures. Because of this I set out to write each poem without worrying about the connection between the content and the selected extinct animal, knowing that the animal would subtly work itself into the writing anyway. This certainly took place, as each poem ended up being a form of elegy for some lost, bright, vivid thing. For some of the poems this was more oblique, painful love affairs or disappearing experiences of the natural world, but for "Flame Brocade Moth" it was more straightforward. The poem is an elegy for someone who is gone, and in it I hoped to capture something of her extraordinary material intensity, her closeness to the teeming world of nonhuman things. It seemed absolutely right for her poem to be linked up with the flame brocade moth, something lost but still burning fiercely at the edges of our understanding.'

JACK UNDERWOOD was born in 1984. His debut collection *Happiness* was published by Faber in 2015. He works as a lecturer at Goldsmiths College and reviews new work for *Poetry London* and *The Poetry Review*. He is currently writing a non-fiction book on the subject of uncertainty. He writes, 'I've always loved Lorca's line "The world's waterspout of / objects various and ready" (depending on translation); it's a wonderful, quietly awestruck way of addressing the fact that there's just too much stuff to consider. I don't remember writing the poem, but I think I probably had this idea in mind, along with the idea that a poem can also be one of those "various objects", and more generally, that all poems are.'

MARK WALDRON's first collection, *The Brand New Dark*, was published by Salt in 2008, his second, *The Itchy Sea*, came out in September 2011. His work appears in *Identity Parade: New British and Irish Poets* (Bloodaxe 2010), and *Best British Poetry 2012, 2013, 2014* and *2015* (all Salt). He's a Poetry Book Society 2014 Next Generation Poet. Mark comments, 'A few months ago I was interviewed about this poem by Francine Elena for praccrit.com, so most of what I say about it now I've probably already said in that interview! One thing I know I mentioned is that I constructed Manning partly because I wanted a character who could act like an idiot in my poems so that I didn't have to act like an idiot in them. I have an overpowering urge sometimes to write in a kind of arch, over-the-top, semi-nonsense style even though I'm well aware that people might find it annoying. To be honest I find it a bit annoying myself. Anyway my clever plan was that I'd force Manning to talk in that affected tone so people would blame him rather than blame me. I thought I could have my cake and Manning could eat it or something.

'Also this poem's concerned with an obsession of mine about the extent to which the world is our projection – the world and the people in it. Marcie is a fictional muse. Muses are usually real people obviously, with a poet's fantasy projected onto them – so they're partly fictional. There's clearly a kind of denying of another's reality in the traditional muse relationship. I wanted to create a fictional character with absolutely no reality, with no flesh and blood human being behind her. That's what poor old Marcie is, she's entirely fictional and it's the reason there's no *so sorry dirt at all for me to make my home in* as it says in the poem. Everything in the poem (and in a way all poems) is made up. Not just Marcie, but Manning, and the moon and the whole world that's seen as being made of blown glass. The section about the blood is a little story about the generous non-solipsistic work of the body in contrast with the solipsistic work of the projecting individual.'

MEGAN WATKINS grew up in Wales and lives with her children in London. She studied Fine Art and works in arts administration. She has published a lot of poems individually in magazines and anthologies. She comes from a printing family and has experimented with collaboration and hand-printed 'broadsides' as a mode of production – an example of which can be seen here: http://akermandaly.com/book/sing-2013/. She writes, 'This was written quite quickly and didn't change much from first draft except to try to pace it formally and give the voice some weight. The first poetry I loved was Anne Sexton's about her children; she is a big influence on how I think about ambivalence, narcissism and unreliable narrators. My thoughts about this poem probably don't bear much relation to how other people read it; it doesn't really matter as a reader what is true or who is unreliable, you respond to the lyric or story. It is the writer who is concerned with the poem as record, with some idea of responsibility and truth.'

KAREN McCARTHY WOOLF, born in London to English and Jamaican parents, is the recipient of the Glenna Luschei *Prairie Schooner* Prize and an AHRC doctoral scholarship at Royal Holloway, University of London, where she is researching new ways of writing about loss, nature and the city. *An Aviary of Small Birds* is a Forward Prize Best First Collection nominee and is published by Carcanet. She writes, '*An Aviary of Small Birds* centres around a single, autobiographical event: a full-term stillbirth at which I lost my baby son Otto. "Mort Dieu" is a sonnet with a Petrarchan rhyme scheme, with two syllables per line. I didn't start out writing a sonnet – I was more interested at that point in syllabics, and I worked my way down from six, to five, then four then the final two. It is an early poem, both in terms of its narrative and compositional chronology. In the book it sits next to a "companion" piece, "Morbleu". At the time, just a few months after the bereavement, I was acutely sensitive to sound. I think this may be a very primal response to trauma: where we are protected from the shock and resulting dreamlike state through a heightening of the senses. "Morbleu" is a poem driven by sound and this is echoed in the formal structure of "Mort Dieu". The two syllables give the poem a binary, bell-like toll – to me it is the book's death knell.

'Reading through my early drafts in my notebook, I noticed the phrase "scream blue murder" – a rather clichéd, idiomatic expression, that nonetheless made me wonder how it had come about. *Brewer's Dictionary of Phrase & Fable* reveals that "blue murder" is an Anglicisation of the French "Morbleu"/"blue death" which in turn is a euphemism for "Mort-Dieu"/"God's death".

'"Mort Dieu" also owes a debt to another longstanding form: the letter. Inherently it carries with it the ghost of call and response, a predominantly conversational tone and an urge to ask questions, whether rhetorical or literal, answered or forgotten. It is also the vehicle through which the test of faith, in humanity, in god, in a sense of justice in the world, can be addressed. The poem is physically slight, and to me this symbolises the very fine line between sentimentality and sentiment that a book about losing that most precious and innocent thing, a newborn baby, must tread.'

SAMANTHA WYNNE-RHYDDERCH's two Picador collections, *Not in These Shoes* and *Banjo* were both shortlisted for Wales Book of the Year. Samantha has held residencies at the Dylan Thomas Boathouse and at the National Wool Museum. In 2014 her pamphlet *Lime & Winter* was published by Rack Press and shortlisted for the Michael Marks Award. She is the recipient of a Hawthornden Fellowship and a Creative Wales Award. Samantha runs a writers' retreat on the Wales coastal path at writebythecoast.co.uk. She comments, 'I'm the kind of writer who relishes stepping into the shoes of a range of characters, trying on the clothes of men and women from different historical periods. To me it feels like acting without having to get on the stage. In my third collection, *Banjo*, I donned the uniforms and furs of the crew of three Antarctic expeditions from the turn of the last century, exploring in verse the role that music and the theatre played in keeping up morale in a challenging environment. Last year I published a pamphlet, *Lime & Winter*, in which I tried on the voices of weavers whom I'd either interviewed or whose working lives I'd researched during a Leverhulme-funded residency at the National Wool Museum. Here I examine two seemingly unrelated subjects (fishing and dementia) by imagining myself as a fisherman's daughter (though my own father neither fished nor suffered from dementia) by following the trajectory of how one person's slow loss of language and memory can sharpen another's relationship to their own language and memories.'

LIST OF MAGAZINES

Ambit
Staithe House, Main Road,
Brancaster Staithe, Norfolk, PE31
8BP
ambitmagazine.co.uk
Poetry editors: Liz Berry and
Declan Ryan

Blackbox Manifold
manifold.group.shef.ac.uk
Editors: Alex Houen and Adam
Piette

B O D Y
bodyliterature.com
Editors: Christopher Crawford,
Stephan Delbos, Joshua Mensch,
Michael Stein

clinic
clinicpresents.com
editors: Sam Buchan-Watts,
Rachael Allen, Sean Roy Parker,
Andrew Parkes

The Dark Horse
3A Blantyre Mill Road, Bothwell,
South Lanarkshire, G71 8DD
thedarkhorsemagazine.com
Editor: Gerry Cambridge

Five Dials
fivedials.com
Editor: Craig Taylor

For Every Year
foreveryyear.eu
Editor: Crispin Best

Granta
12 Addison Avenue, London
W11 4QR
granta.com
Poetry editor: Rachael Allen

Ink, Sweat & Tears
inksweatandtears.co.uk
Editor: Helen Ivory

The Learned Pig
thelearnedpig.org
Poetry editor: Crystal Bennes

Lighthouse
gatehousepress.com/lighthouse
Poetry editors: Meirion Jordan, Jo
Surzyn, Julia Webb

Litmus
litmuspublishing.co.uk
Editors: Elinor Cleghorn and
Dorothy Lehane

London Review of Books
28 Little Russell Street, London
WC1A 2HN
lrb.co.uk
Editor: Mary-Kay Wilmers

Long Poem Magazine
20 Spencer Rise, London, NW5
1AP
longpoemmagazine.org.uk
Editors: Linda Black and Lucy
Hamilton

Modern Poetry in Translation
mptmagazine.com
Editor: Sasha Dugdale

Morning Star
William Rust House, 52 Beachy
Road, London E3 2NS
morningstaronline.co.uk
Poetry editor: Jody Porter

New Statesman
John Carpenter House, 7
Carmelite Street, London EC4Y
0BS
newstatesman.co.uk
Poetry editor: Tom Gatti

Oxford Poetry
Magdalen College, Oxford, OX1
4AU
oxfordpoetry.co.uk
Editors: Mika Ross-Southall,
Lavinia Singer, Andrew Wynn-
Owen

PN Review
4th Floor, Alliance House, 30
Cross Street, Manchester M2
7AQ
pnreview.co.uk
Editor: Michael Schmidt

Poem
c/o Durham University
Department of English Studies,
Hallgarth House, 77 Hallgarth
Street, Durham City DH1 3AY
Editor: Fiona Sampson

Poems in Which
poemsinwhich.com
Editors: Nia Davies, Wayne
Holloway-Smith, Amy Key, Alex
MacDonald, Rebecca Perry

Poetry London
The Albany, Douglas Way,
Deptford, London SE8 4AG
poetrylondon.co.uk
Editor: Ahren Warner

The Poetry Paper
The Poetry Trust, 9 New Cut,
Halesworth, Suffolk IP19 8BY
Editor: Dean Parkin

The Poetry Review
The Poetry Society, 22 Betterton
Street, London WC2H 9BX
Editor: Maurice Riordan

Poetry Wales
57 Nolton Street, Bridgend CF31
3AE
poetrywales.co.uk
Editor: Nia Davies

Prac Crit
praccrit.com
Editors: Dai George, Sarah Howe,
Vidyan Ravinthiran

The Quietus
The Lexington, 96–98 Pentonville
Road, London N1 9JB
thequietus.com
Poetry editor: Karl Smith

The Rialto
PO Box 309, Aylsham, Norwich
NR11 6LN
therialto.co.uk
Editor: Michael Mackmin

Tears in the Fence
Portman Lodge, Durweston,
Blandford Forum, Dorset DT11
0QA
tearsinthefence.om
Editor: David Caddy

tender
tenderjournal.co.uk
Editors: Rachael Allen and Sophie
Collins

Test Centre Magazine
77a Greenwood Road, London
E8 1NT
testcentre.co.uk
Editor: Will Shutes

Times Literary Supplement
The News Building, 1 London
Bridge Street, London SE1 9GF
the-tls.co.uk
Poetry editor: Alan Jenkins

Shearsman
50 Westons Hill Drive, Emersons
Green, Bristol BS16 7DF
shearsman.com
Editor: Tony Frazer

Sonofabook
cbeditions.com/magazine.html
Editor: Charles Boyle

Vada
vadamagazine.co.uk
Poetry editor: Adam Lowe

Wasafiri
The Open University in London,
1–11 Hawley Crescent, London
NW1 8NP
wasafiri.org
Editor: Shusheila Nasta

The White Review
243 Knightsbridge, London SW7
1DN
thewhitereview.org
Editors: Benjamin Eastham and
Jacques Testard

The Wolf
wolfmagazine.co.uk
Editors: James Byrne and Sandeep
Parmar

ACKNOWLEDGEMENTS

Grateful acknowledgement is made to the publications from which the poems in this volume were chosen. Unless specifically noted otherwise, copyright to the poems is held by the individual poets.

Aria Aber: 'First Generation Immigrant Child' appeared in *Wasafiri*. Reprinted by permission of the poet.

Astrid Alben: 'One of the Guys' appeared in the *Times Literary Supplement*. Reprinted by permission of the poet.

Rachael Allen: 'Prawns of Joe' appeared in the *Test Centre Magazine* and *The Quietus*. Reprinted by permission of the poet.

Janette Ayachi: 'On Keeping a Wolf' appeared in *Oxford Poetry*. Reprinted by permission of the poet.

Tara Bergin: 'The Hairdresser' appeared in the *Times Literary Supplement*. Reprinted by permission of the poet.

Crispin Best: 'poem in which I mention at the last minute an orrery' appeared in *Poems in Which*. Reprinted by permission of the poet.

A.K. Blakemore: 'Poem in which darlings' appeared in *Poems in Which*. Reprinted by permission of the poet.

Sarah Boulton: 'Powder' appeared in *tender*. Reprinted by permission of the poet.

Kit Buchan: 'The Man Whom I Bitterly Hate' appeared in *Five Dials*. Reprinted by permission of the poet.

Sam Buchan-Watts: 'The days go just like that' appeared in *Poetry London*. Reprinted by permission of the poet.

Miles Burrows: 'Letter to an Elderly Poet' appeared in *PN Review*. Reprinted by permission of the poet.

Niall Campbell: 'Midnight' appeared in *Poetry London*. Reprinted by permission of the poet.

Vahni Capildeo: 'Moss, for Maya' appeared in *clinic*. Reprinted by permission of the poet.

Kayo Chingonyi: 'Legerdemain' appeared in the *Morning Star* and *Campaign in Poetry* (The Emma Press, 2015). Reprinted by permission of the poet.

Sophie Collins: 'Dear No. 24601' appeared in *The White Review* and *Can I Borrow a Feeling?* (Clinic, 2015). Reprinted by permission of the poet.

Claire Crowther: 'Week of Flies, 1968' appeared in *Shearsman*. Reprinted by permission of the poet.

Paula Cunningham: 'A History of Snow' appeared in *PN Review*. Reprinted by permission of the poet.

Jesse Darling: '14 Dreams' appeared (as 'Eleven Dreams') in *tender*. Reprinted by permission of the poet.

Patricia Debney: 'Dream 1' appeared in *Litmus*. Reprinted by permission of the poet.

Ian Duhig: 'The Rûm District' appeared in *The Poetry Review*. Reprinted by permission of the poet.

Joe Dunthorne: 'The Old Days' appeared in the *London Review of Books*. Reprinted by permission of the poet.

Francine Elena: 'Fish Magic' appeared in *Poetry London*. Reprinted by permission of the poet.

Inua Ellams: 'Swallow Twice' appeared in *Oxford Poetry* and *Ten: The New Wave* (Bloodaxe, 2014). Reprinted by permission of the poet.

Andrew Elliott: 'The Storm in American Fiction' appeared in *Sonofabook*. Reprinted by permission of the poet.

Victoria Field: 'Mrs Bagnall Explains Magnesium' appeared in *The Dark Horse*. Reprinted by permission of the poet.

Annie Freud: 'Birth Control' appeared in *Poetry London* and was collected in *The Remains* (Picador, 2015). Reprinted by permission of the poet and publisher.

Matthew Gregory: 'Decline of the House—' appeared in *Ambit*. Reprinted by permission of the poet.

David Hart: 'He wrote' appeared in *The Poetry Review*. Reprinted by permission of the poet.

Selima Hill: 'My Father's Smile' appeared in *The Poetry Paper* and was collected in *Jutland* (Bloodaxe, 2015). Reprinted by permission of the poet and publisher.

Sarah Howe: 'Sirens' appeared in *The Poetry Review* and was collected in *Loop of Jade* (Chatto, 2015). Reprinted by permission of the poet and publisher.

Kathleen Jamie: 'The Berries' appeared in the *New Statesman* and was collected in *The Bonniest Companie* (Picador, 2015). Reprinted by permission of the poet and publisher.

Tom Jenks: *from* 'Spruce' appeared in *The Wolf* and was collected in *Spruce* (Blart Books, 2015). Reprinted by permission of the poet.

Luke Kennard: 'Cain Anagrams' appeared in *The Learned Pig*. Reprinted by permission of the poet.

Amy Key: 'Gillingham' appeared in the *Morning Star*. Reprinted by permission of the poet.

Kate Kilalea: 'Sometimes I think the world is just a vast breeding ground for mosquitoes' appeared in *tender*. Reprinted by permission of the poet.

Caleb Klaces: 'Genit—' appeared in *The White Review*. Reprinted by permission of the poet.

Zaffar Kunial: 'The Word' appeared in *The Poetry Review* and was collected in his Faber New Poets pamphlet. Reprinted by permission of the poet and publisher.

Daisy Lafarge: 'girl vs. sincerity' appeared in *clinic*. Reprinted by permission of the poet.

Melissa Lee-Houghton: 'i am very precious' appeared in *Prac Crit*. Reprinted by permission of the poet.

Dorothy Lehane: 'Sombrero galaxy' appeared in *Tears in the Fence* and was collected in *Ephemeris* (Nine Arches, 2014). Reprinted by permission of the poet.

Fran Lock: 'Melpomene' appeared in *The Poetry Review*. Reprinted by permission of the poet.

Adam Lowe: 'Vada That' appeared in *Vada Magazine (Dog Horn Publishing)* and *Ten: The New Wave* (Bloodaxe, 2014). Reprinted by permission of the poet.

Chris McCabe: 'The Repossessor' appeared in *The Wolf*. Reprinted by permission of the poet.

Amy McCauley: 'Kadmea Touch Me' appeared in *The Rialto*. Reprinted by permission of the poet.

Alex MacDonald: 'End Space' appeared in *Poetry London*. Reprinted by permission of the poet.

Andrew McMillan, 'Ókunna Þér Runna' appeared in *Modern Poetry in Translation* and was collected in *physical* (Cape, 2015). Reprinted by permission of the poet and publisher.

Kathryn Maris: 'It was discovered that gut bacteria were responsible' appeared in *Granta*. Reprinted by permission of the poet.

Sophie Mayer: 'Silence, Singing' appeared in *The Wolf* and was collected in *(O)* (Arc, 2015) Reprinted by permission of the poet and publisher.

Kim Moore: 'The Knowing' appeared in *Poem* and was collected in *The Art of Falling* (Seren, 2015). Reprinted by permission of the poet and publisher.

Salah Niazi: 'The Dilemma of Al-Kamali' appeared in *Long Poem Magazine*. Reprinted by permission of the poet.

Jeremy Over: 'Artifically Arranged Scenes' appeared in *PN Review*. Reprinted by permission of the poet.

Bobby Parker: 'Thank You for Swallowing My Cum' appeared in *B O D Y*. Reprinted by permission of the poet.

Rebecca Perry: 'apples are ¼ air' appeared in *For Every Year*. Reprinted by permission of the poet.

Holly Pester: 'The man from Okay' appeared in *The White Review*. Reprinted by permission of the poet.

Heather Phillipson: 'Guess what?' appeared in *Poetry London*. Reprinted by permission of the poet.

Padraig Regan: 'Apples, Cherries, Apricots & Other Fruits in a Basket, with Pears, Plums, Robins, a Woodpecker, a Parrot, & a Monkey Eating Nuts on a Table' appeared in *The Poetry Review*. Reprinted by permission of the poet.

Sam Riviere: 'Preferences' appeared in *The Poetry Review*. Reprinted by permission of the poet.

Sophie Robinson: 'where the heart is streaming' appeared in the *Morning Star*. Reprinted by permission of the poet.

Jessica Schouela: 'Poem In Which I Watch Jane Brakhage Give Birth' appeared in *Poems in Which*. Reprinted by permission of the poet.

Stephen Sexton: 'Elegy for Olive Oyl' appeared in *Poetry London* and was collected in *Oils* (The Emma Press, 2014). Reprinted by permission of the poet and publisher.

Penelope Shuttle: 'O Blinde Augen' appeared in *The Rialto*. Reprinted by permission of the poet.

Hannah Silva: *from* 'The Kathy Doll' appeared in *Blackbox Manifold*. Reprinted by permission of the poet.

Marcus Slease: 'The Underground' appeared in *Lighthouse*. Reprinted by permission of the poet.

Greta Stoddart: 'Letter from Sido' appeared in *The Poetry Review* and was collected in *Alive Alive O* (Bloodaxe, 2015). Reprinted by permission of the poet and publisher.

Chloe Stopa-Hunt: 'The Leopard-God' appeared in *clinic*. Reprinted by permission of the poet.

Rebecca Tamás: 'Flame Brocade Moth' appeared in *B O D Y*. Reprinted by permission of the poet.

Jack Underwood: 'Accidental Narratives' appeared in the *New Statesman* and was collected in *Happiness* (Faber & Faber, 2015). Reprinted by permission of the poet.

Mark Waldron: 'I am lordly, puce and done' appeared in *Prac Crit*. Reprinted by permission of the poet.

Megan Watkins: 'Losing Lion' appeared in *Poetry Wales*. Reprinted by permission of the poet.

Karen McCarthy Woolf: 'Mort Dieu' appeared in *Ink, Sweat & Tears* and was collected in *An Aviary of Small Birds*. Reprinted by permission of the poet and publisher.

Samantha Wynne-Rhydderch: 'Losing It' appeared in *Poetry London*. Reprinted by permission of the poet.

ALSO AVAILABLE FROM SALT

ALSO AVAILABLE
FROM SALT

ELIZABETH BAINES
Too Many Magpies (9781844717217)
The Birth Machine (9781907773020)

LESLEY GLAISTER
Little Egypt (9781907773723)

ALISON MOORE
The Lighthouse (9781907773174)
The PreWar House and Other Stories (9781907773501)
He Wants (9781907773815)

ALICE THOMPSON
Justine (9781784630324)
The Falconer (9781784630096)
The Existential Detective (9781784630119)
Burnt Island (9781907773488)

MEIKE ZIERVOGEL
Magda (9781907773402)
Clara's Daughter (9781907773792)
Kauthar (9781784630294)

NEXT GENERATION POETS AT SALT

TOBIAS HILL
Year of the Dog (9781844715534)
Midnight in the City of Clocks (9781844715497)
Zoo (9781844714131)
Nocturne in Chrome & Sunset Yellow (1844712621)

LUKE KENNARD
The Solex Brothers (Redux) (9781844715480)
The Harbour Beyond the Movie (9781844715336)
The Migraine Hotel (9781844715558)
A Lost Expression (9781844718757)

MARK WALDRON
The Brand New Dark (9781844718177)
The Itchy Sea (9781844718276)